Specials!

Sustainable design

Jan Llewellyn, Trish Colley and Paul Anderson

Acknowledgements

The authors would like to thank Ian Capewell, Practical Action's Design and Technology Education Officer, for his support and advice during the writing process.

Trish Colley would like to acknowledge help and support received from staff at Beverley High School.

P. 32 © The make-me wheel reproduced with kind permission from the Education Unit at Practical Action; p. 42 © 2009 Fairtrade Foundation; p. 62 © Lofthouse, V. A and Bhamra T., Ecodesign web. 2000, Cranfield University. www.informationinspiration.org.uk

---

© 2009 Folens Limited, on behalf of the authors.

United Kingdom: Folens Publishers, Waterslade House, Thame Road, Haddenham, Buckinghamshire, HP17 8NT.
Email: folens@folens.com   Website: www.folens.com

Ireland: Folens Publishers, Greenhills Road, Tallaght, Dublin 24.
Email: info@folens.ie   Website: www.folens.ie

Folens publications are protected by international copyright laws. All rights are reserved. The copyright of all materials in this publication, except where otherwise stated, remains the property of the publisher and the authors. No part of this publication may be reproduced, stored in a retrieval system, or transmitted, in any form or by any means, for whatever purpose, without the written permission of Folens Limited, except where authorized.

Folens allows photocopying of pages marked 'copiable page' for educational use, providing that this use is within the confines of the purchasing institution. Copiable pages should not be declared in any return in respect of any photocopying licence.

Jan Llewellyn, Trish Colley and Paul Anderson hereby assert their moral rights to be identified as the authors of this work in accordance with the Copyright, Designs and Patents Act 1988.

Commissioning editor: Paul Naish   Editor: Cathy Hurren
Text design and layout: Planman   Illustrator: Sarah Deakin/www.hardwickstudios.com
Cover design: Holbrook Design   Cover image: © iStockphoto.com/PatrickCoalka

The websites recommended in this publication were correct at the time of going to press, however, websites may have been removed or web addresses changed since that time. Folens has made every attempt to suggest websites that are reliable and appropriate for student's use. It is not unknown for unscrupulous individuals to put unsuitable material on websites that may be accessed by students. Teachers should check all websites before allowing students to access them. Folens is not responsible for the content of external websites.

For general spellings Folens adheres to the *Oxford Dictionary of English*, Second Edition (Revised), 2005.

First published 2009 by Folens Limited.

Every effort has been made to contact copyright holders of material used in this publication. If any copyright holder has been overlooked, we will be pleased to make any necessary arrangements.

British Library Cataloguing in Publication Data. A catalogue record for this publication is available from the British Library.

ISBN 978-1-85008-467-9   Folens code FD4679

Contents

Introduction	4
The 6Rs	5
What are the 6Rs?	6
How are the 6Rs used?	7
Why repair?	8
Clothes	9
Repairing clothes	10
Reduce	11
Reducing materials and energy	12
The need for packaging	13
Can we use less?	14
Problem-solving	15
Getting the shopping home	16
Recycle	17
Rubbish audit	18
What else could we recycle?	19
Recycle Snap!	20
Recycling paper	21
Recycled handmade paper	22
Reuse	23
What can you do with me?	24
Am I rubbish?	25
Is it waste?	26
Leftover food	27
Hibernation home	28
Rethink	29
Ways to rethink	30
Eco-eggs	31
The make-me wheel	32
Walk to school campaign	33
Green skateboarding	34

Refuse	35
Needs and wants	36
Sustainable alternatives	37
Packaged sandwiches	38
Shoes	39
Ethical trade	40
Fair trade	41
What is fair trade?	42
Where in the world?	43
That's not fair!	44
A lovely cup of coffee	45
Chocolate heaven	46
Renewable energy	47
Electricity	48
What is renewable energy?	49
Wind power	50
Solar power	51
Eco-friendly homes	52
Alternative choices	53
Alternative choices	54
Material choices	55
Transport choices	56
Build a land yacht	57
Product life cycles	58
Product life cycles	59
Carbon footprint	60
Lose your bottle	61
The eco-web	62
The end?	63
Assessment sheet	64

Introduction

Specials! Design and Technology activities are planned for students with a reading comprehension age of seven to nine years and working at levels 1 to 3. This book is divided into activities that underpin the central concepts of sustainable design, for example, the 6Rs, fair trade, product life cycles and alternative energy. Students are guided through essential activities to help them consider sustainability issues when designing and making.

This book contains ten separate units covering the topics needed to complete the theme of the book. Each unit has one or more photocopiable Resource sheets and several Activity sheets. This allows the teacher to work in different ways. The tasks are differentiated throughout the book and offer all students the opportunity to expand their skills.

The teacher can work in different ways: each unit could be taught as one or two lessons with students working individually, in pairs or in groups. Alternatively, a single Resource sheet and the related Activity sheet(s) could be used as required. Some student pages are more challenging than others so they will need to be selected accordingly.

The Teacher's notes give guidance and are laid out as follows:

Objectives
These are the main skills or knowledge to be learnt.

Prior knowledge
This refers to the minimum skills or knowledge required by students to complete the tasks. Some Activity sheets are more challenging than others and will need to be selected accordingly.

Links
All units link to the Design and Technology National Curriculum at Key Stage 3, Scottish attainment targets, and the Northern Ireland and Welsh Programmes of Study.

Background
This gives additional information for the teacher about particular aspects of the topic.

Starter activity
Since the units can be taught as a lesson, a warm-up activity focusing on an aspect of the unit is suggested.

Resource sheets and Activity sheets
The Resource sheets are used as stimulus for discussion and contain no tasks or activities. Where useful, keywords are given in the Teacher's notes and related tasks are provided on the Activity sheets. Links with other Activity sheets are sometimes indicated.

Plenary
The teacher can use the suggestions here to do additional work, recap on the main points covered, or reinforce a particular point.

Assessment sheet
At the end of the book there is an Assessment sheet focusing on student progress and learning. It can be used in different ways. A student could complete it as a self-assessment, while the teacher or support assistant also completes one on the student's progress. The two can then be compared and contrasted during a discussion. Alternatively, students could work in pairs to carry out a peer-assessment and then compare outcomes.

Look out for other titles in the Design and Technology series, including:

- Designing and making
- Food
- Food 2
- Graphic products
- Product design
- Resistant materials
- Systems and control
- Textiles
- Textiles 2

Teacher's notes

The 6Rs

Objectives
- To learn what the 6Rs are
- To explain what is meant by repair and how this contributes to sustainability
- To show how the life of textile goods can be extended

Prior knowledge
Students should be aware of the meaning of sustainability, the term environmentally friendly and 'green' activities.

NC links
Key concepts: 1.1 Designing and making; 1.4 Critical evaluation
Key processes: d, f, h
Range and content: a, c, d
Curriculum opportunities: a, b

Northern Ireland PoS
Communicating: a, b
Designing: b

Scottish attainment targets
Technology: Needs and how they are met: Level E
Resources and how they are managed: Level D
Processes and how they are applied: Level D

Welsh PoS
Skills: Designing: 8
Skills: Making: 15

Starter activity
In small groups, students should try to list as many ways they can be environmentally friendly as possible.

Resource sheets and Activity sheets
The Activity sheet, 'What are the 6Rs?', explains what the 6Rs are (rethink, reuse, recycle, repair, reduce and refuse). Students are encouraged to identify each of the 6Rs with an explanation of what each one means.

The Activity sheet, 'How are the 6Rs used?', encourages students to consider what products or activities would fall into each category in order to help them understand the differences between the 6Rs.

The Activity sheet, 'Why repair?', asks students to focus on one particular aspect of the 6Rs: repair. This will help to reinforce the advantages of repairing products rather than replacing them.

Students are asked to consider the amount of clothing that is thrown away by using the Activity sheet, 'Clothes'. Students are required to investigate how and why people dispose of clothing.

Using the Activity sheet, 'Repairing clothes', students are encouraged to consider functional approaches to repairing clothing, along with aesthetic considerations such as customization. They are then encouraged to think independently and customize an item of clothing that is in need of repair.

Plenary
In small groups, students should look at different types of clothing and explain what could be done to extend their life, whilst still keeping them attractive to the user.

Background

This unit introduces students to the thinking behind the concept of the 6Rs as a way of guiding them to improve sustainability in the design, use and manufacture of products. In particular it aims to encourage students to consider how they can use 'repair' to extend the life of a product so that fewer new materials are required, in order to help the environment.

Activity sheet – The 6Rs

What are the 6Rs?

The 6Rs are things that need to be thought about when designing, making and using products. This is so they can become more sustainable.

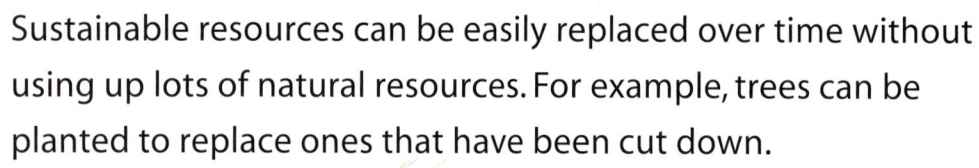

Sustainable resources can be easily replaced over time without using up lots of natural resources. For example, trees can be planted to replace ones that have been cut down.

☞ Draw an arrow from each of the 6Rs to match them to their correct description.

1 **R**ethink	Cut down on the amount of energy or materials that are used to make a product.
2 **R**euse	Refuse to use products you don't need or refuse to use products that are not made from sustainable resources.
3 **R**ecycle	Instead of throwing a product away because it has stopped working, repair it!
4 **R**epair	Take an existing product that you might replace with something new or just throw away, and reuse the material or parts of the product for another purpose.
5 **R**educe	Rethink products that you buy or design. For example: • Do you really need to buy something new? • Is the product made from sustainable resources? • Can it be reused or redesigned to make it more environmentally friendly?
6 **R**efuse	Take an existing product that has become waste and reprocess the material for use in a new product. Or put it in a recycling bin for someone else to reprocess.

Activity sheet – The 6Rs

How are the 6Rs used?

Many designers, manufacturers and consumers use the 6Rs to help make products more environmentally friendly. Even using just one of the 6Rs can have a big effect on a product and how it is used.

☞ Each of the following products or activities have been affected by one of the 6Rs. Cut them out and match them to one of the 6R categories.

A dress made from natural materials	Mending a car
A newspaper made from old paper	Food with less packaging
Use low-energy light bulbs	Mend rather than throw away

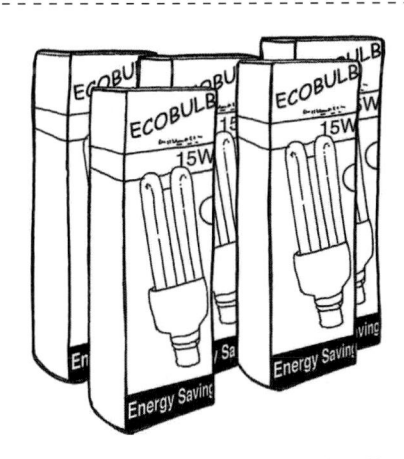

© Folens (copiable page)   Sustainable design

Activity sheet – The 6Rs

Why repair?

Products sometimes stop being able to do the job they were needed for. For example, cars break down and clothes get holes in them.

Products are often thrown away or replaced with a new version. This can cost a lot of money and use up a lot of materials. Repairing something means it will last longer, so you save money and use fewer materials.

☞ 1 Use the word bank to complete the following sentences.

　a If a computer monitor is damaged, it costs _____ to buy a new monitor than to buy a _____ computer.

　b If a page of a book is torn, it is cheaper to _____ it than to buy a new book.

　c If a product is repaired, fewer _____ are used.

Word bank
● repair　　● less　　● new　　● materials

Different ways to repair products can include:

- Sewing clothes together or patching them
- Joining together broken parts using glue or screws
- Replacing broken or worn out parts.

☞ 2 Complete the following table by writing down how each product could be repaired. An example has been given to help you.

Product	How it might be repaired
A broken vase	Glue the broken parts back together.
A coat with a hole in the elbow	
A car with a flat tyre	
An MP3 player with a flat battery	

Activity sheet – The 6Rs

Clothes

Every year, the average person in the UK throws out over 30kg of clothes and shoes. Some of this is given to charity shops, but most of it is thrown in the bin. The reasons clothes are thrown away include:

- They are no longer fashionable
- People grow out of them
- They wear out
- They get damaged.

☞ Make a list of all of the clothes you and your family have given or thrown away in the last year. Write down what happened to each item of clothing and the reason why it was thrown out.

Item of clothing	What happened to it?	Why was it thrown out?

Activity sheet – The 6Rs

Repairing clothes

Damaged clothes can be repaired in lots of ways. For example, splits or tears can be sewn up and patches can be ironed or sewn on.

Colours can also be changed by dyeing them. This can be a good way to customize your clothes and make them unique.

☞ On the coat below, add patches to repair any damage and make it a unique, fashionable item that you would wear.

Teacher's notes

Reduce

Objectives

- To understand that products can be over-packaged
- To understand that products have a life cycle
- To use strategies that promote the reduction of materials
- To try different ways of designing that help to promote a range of ideas

Prior knowledge

Students should have knowledge of different types of packaging.

NC links

Key concepts: 1.1 Designing and making;
1.4 Critical evaluation
Key processes: h
Range and content: a, b, c, d
Curriculum opportunities: a, b

Northern Ireland PoS

Economic awareness

Scottish attainment targets

Technology: Needs and how they are met: Level C
Resources and how they are managed: Level D

Welsh PoS

Skills: Designing: 2, 4, 8
Skills: Making: 1, 2, 3

Background

The importance of reducing in relation to the 6Rs cannot be stressed enough. Some products' life cycles from retail shelves to landfill sites occur daily, for example, packaged sandwichs, appliances and clothes. In some cases consumers are persuaded to buy the latest must-have product, but do we really need to buy expensive bottled water when we can get drinking water from a tap? This unit will help students to appreciate some of the more extravagant excesses in our daily lives. By questioning the impact of the production of products and their disposal, students will be able to identify the futile life cycles of some products and look creatively at possible solutions that could make a difference.

Starter activity

Students should use the Resource sheet, 'Reducing materials and energy', as a starter activity by matching up products that are similar. Students should be encouraged to think about why there are so many duplicate products available, to question whether they are all needed and what their impact is on the environment.

Resource sheets and Activity sheets

The Activity sheet, 'The need for packaging', looks at the purpose of packaging. Students are to consider the products given on the sheet and rank them in order of what they think is the most important reason for the packaging. They are then asked to consider reasons for other product packaging – this activity could be extended by students bringing in packaging examples of their own. Further information on packaging can be found at the INCPEN (the Industry Council for Packaging and the Environment, www.incpen.org).

Using the Activity sheet, 'Can we use less?', students are asked to consider what happens after products have been used and what could be done to reduce waste. They are then encouraged to create a poster to highlight what could be done to reduce waste.

The Activity sheet, 'Problem-solving', provides students with a challenge: to work out how to transport eggs from a farm to a market so they don't break. As well as the safe transportation element, students may also like to look at the possibility of recycling or reusing materials.

Using the Activity sheet, 'Getting the shopping home', students are to look at alternatives to using plastic carrier bags.

Plenary

Students could be encouraged to carry out further research on reducing waste using the following websites: www.traid.org.uk and Canby, www.canby.co.uk, who produce cotton, hessian and jute bags.

Resource sheet – Reduce

Reducing materials and energy

Activity sheet – Reduce

The need for packaging

👉 1 Rank the following in order of the most important reason for packaging.

Security measures to stop theft	To easily move goods from a factory to a shop
To protect what's inside	So the product looks good
Makes it easier for a consumer to take a product home	Makes it easier to display goods in a shop

👉 2 With a partner, discuss what the most important reasons are for packaging:

- Sandwiches
- Fruit and vegetables
- Easter eggs.

© Folens (copiable page)   Sustainable design

Activity sheet – Reduce

Can we use less?

☞ 1 Write or draw what you think happens to each of the following examples. Then write or draw an idea about what could be done to reduce waste. An example has been given to help you.

A good choice?	What happens next?	What could be done to reduce waste?
A bottle of water	The bottle goes in the bin	Drink tap water
A packaged sandwich		
A teenager's bedroom		
A mobile phone		
Making short journeys		

☞ 2 Design a poster with the heading 'What can we do to reduce waste?'.

14   Sustainable design   © Folens (copiable page)

Activity sheet – Reduce

Problem-solving

A farmer has run out of egg boxes! He needs to take his hens' eggs to sell at the market. He has some old boxes lying around but the eggs will roll around inside them. The eggs could get broken as the road is bumpy.

☞ How could you protect the eggs on their journey to the market?

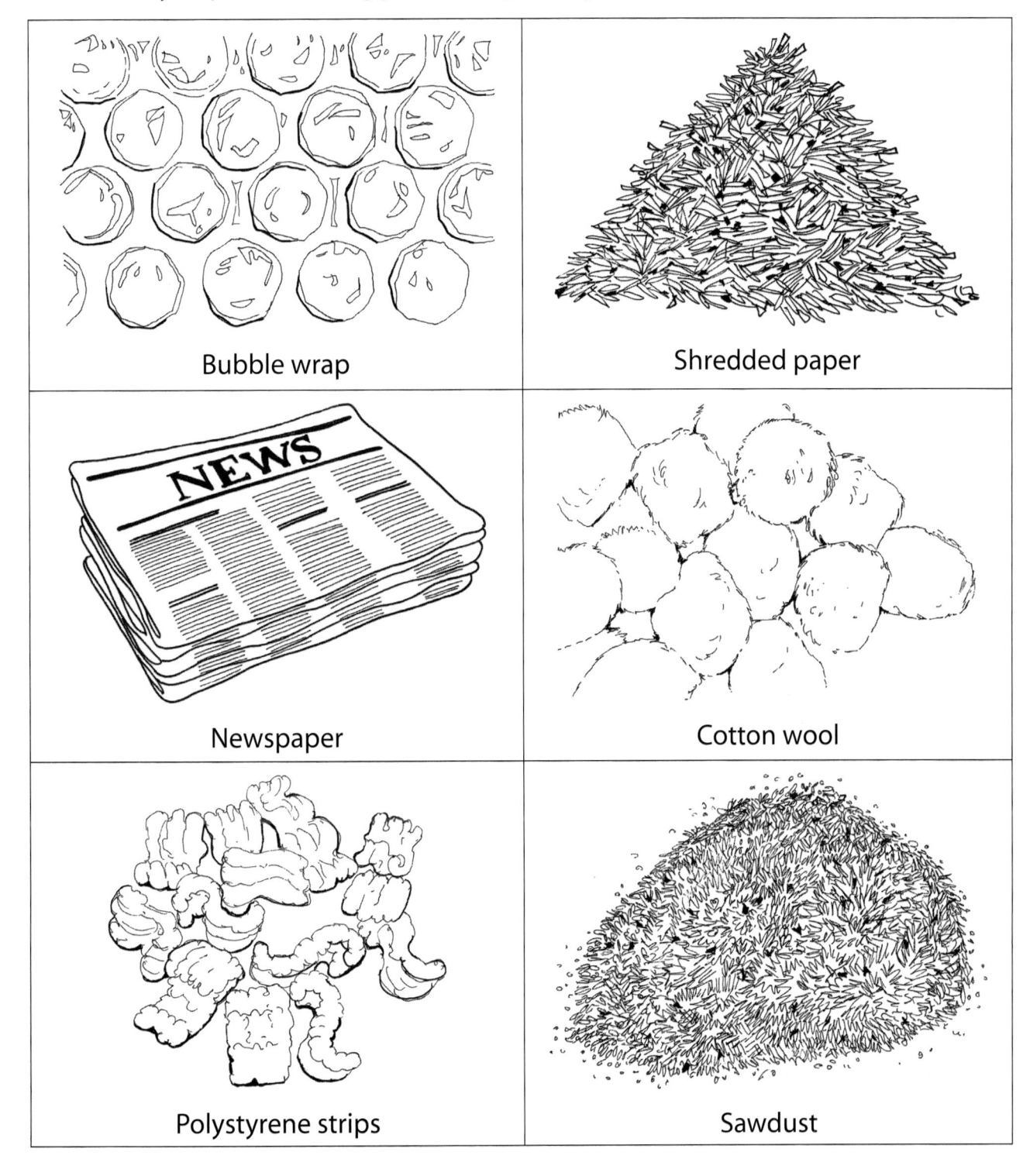

Bubble wrap	Shredded paper
Newspaper	Cotton wool
Polystyrene strips	Sawdust

© Folens (copiable page) Sustainable design 15

Activity sheet – Reduce

Getting the shopping home

👉 1 What would happen if there were no more plastic carrier bags in the world? Write down your ideas in the space below.

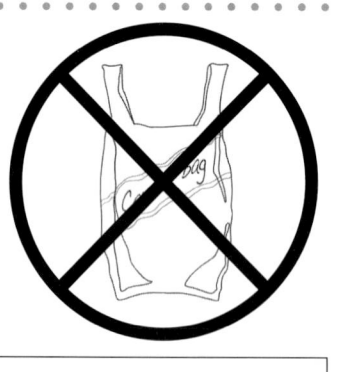

👉 2 Draw a way of improving the following products so you could carry your shopping in them. Write down if you think your ideas are good and why.

Product	Improved product	Is it a good idea?
A bucket		
A basket		
A pair of jeans		

Teacher's notes

Recycle

Objectives

- To look at how products can be recycled
- To understand how a product's life can be extended beyond its initial use
- To use strategies that promote the recycling of materials
- To try different ways of designing that help to promote a range of ideas

Prior knowledge

Students should be familiar with the process of sorting rubbish for recycling purposes.

NC links

Key concepts: 1.1 Designing and making; 1.4 Critical evaluation
Key processes: h
Range and content: a, c, d
Curriculum opportunities: a, b

Northern Ireland PoS

Economic awareness

Scottish attainment targets

Technology: Needs and how they are met: Level C
Resources and how they are managed: Level D

Welsh PoS

Skills: Designing: 2, 4, 8
Skills: Making: 1, 2, 3

Background

Recycling means to take an existing product that has become waste and reprocess the material for use in a new product. Recycling is probably the most familiar of the 6Rs to students as it is something they, or their family, may already do at home.

Starter activity

Students should consider what recycling they do at home. This could be in the form of a class survey or discussion. Students should think about the following questions: do they recycle? If so, what and how do they recycle? Students should go on to ask if we should recycle at all. To do this they need to understand a product's life cycle. For example, a plastic drinks bottle is made from an unsustainable oil source. Put into landfill, it can take up to 1000 years to rot down.

Resource sheets and Activity sheets

The Activity sheet, 'Rubbish audit', asks students to conduct a rubbish audit by considering the places in school where rubbish is dumped. This activity aims to make students more aware of waste that is generated.

The Activity sheet, 'What else could we recycle?', requires students to consider the benefits of recycling an old pair of trainers. This will highlight the need for everyone to recycle old products rather than just throw them away into landfill sites. This activity could lead on to a class debate about the ethical considerations of recycling. Students could consider Worn Again, a company who produce items made of recycled materials (www.wornagain.co.uk).

Students are encouraged to think quickly about items that can be recycled using the Activity sheet, 'Recycle Snap!'. Students can play the game in the same way as traditional Snap, by matching up pairs and calling out 'Snap!'. If a picture is turned over that matches a recycling symbol, students are to call out 'Recycle Snap!'. The cards can be photocopied and laminated to create a reusable resource.

The Activity sheet, 'Recycling paper', looks at using waste paper to create a papier mâché product. This activity aims to highlight to students that by recycling materials, they can create something new.

Students are then asked to consider other products that could be created through the Activity sheet, 'Recycled handmade paper'. To extend this task, students could be encouraged to produce their own handmade paper. The EcoKids website provides some useful resources (www.ecokids.ca/pub/fun_n_games/printables/activities/assets/science_nature/paper_making.pdf).

Plenary

Students could be encouraged to set up a student recycling team to promote and encourage recycling around school.

© Folens — Sustainable design

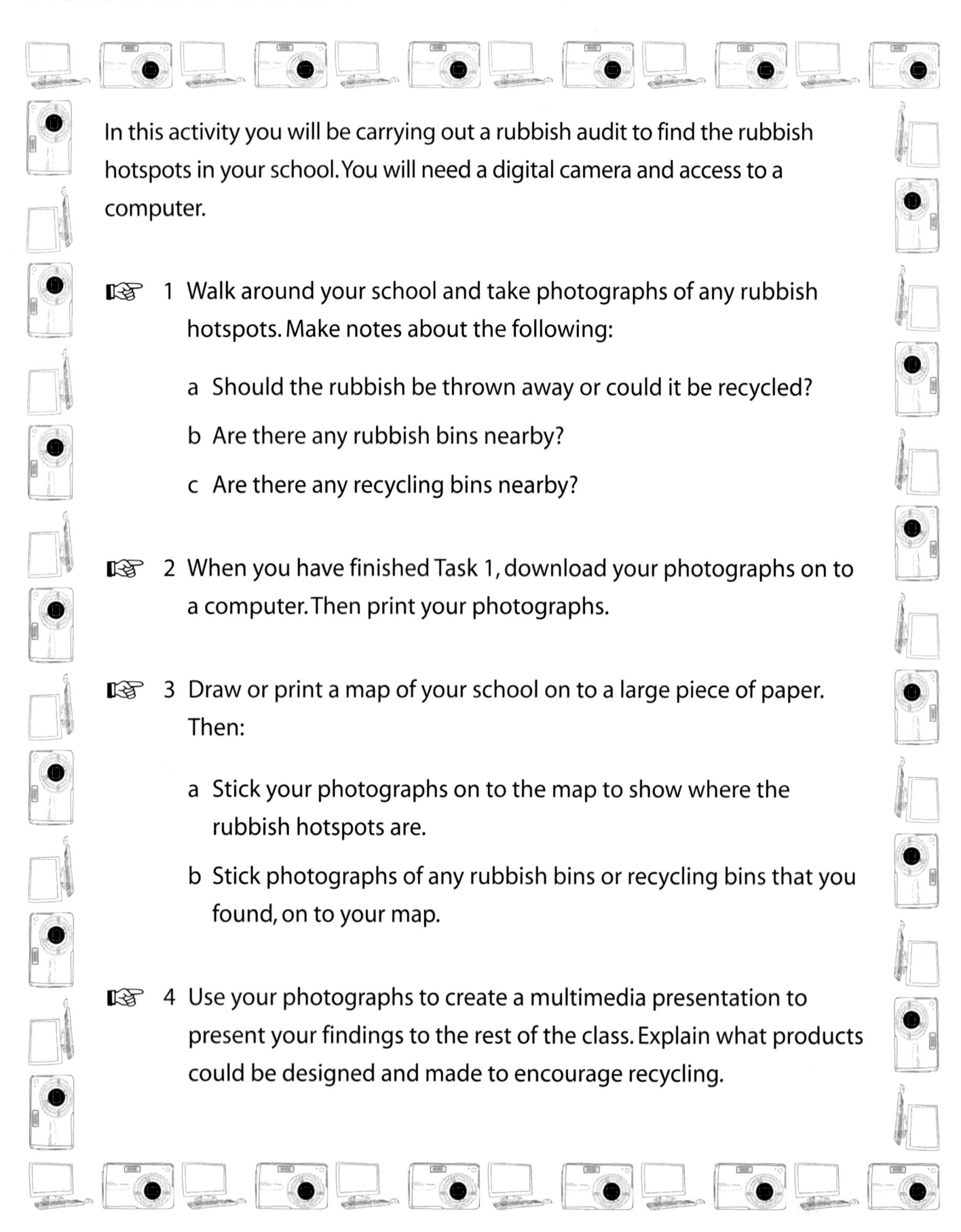

Activity sheet – Recycle

Rubbish audit

In this activity you will be carrying out a rubbish audit to find the rubbish hotspots in your school. You will need a digital camera and access to a computer.

☞ 1 Walk around your school and take photographs of any rubbish hotspots. Make notes about the following:

   a Should the rubbish be thrown away or could it be recycled?

   b Are there any rubbish bins nearby?

   c Are there any recycling bins nearby?

☞ 2 When you have finished Task 1, download your photographs on to a computer. Then print your photographs.

☞ 3 Draw or print a map of your school on to a large piece of paper. Then:

   a Stick your photographs on to the map to show where the rubbish hotspots are.

   b Stick photographs of any rubbish bins or recycling bins that you found, on to your map.

☞ 4 Use your photographs to create a multimedia presentation to present your findings to the rest of the class. Explain what products could be designed and made to encourage recycling.

Activity sheet – Recycle

What else could we recycle?

Every year, 65 million pairs of trainers are sold in the UK. What do you do with your old ones? Did you know that your trainers can be recycled?

☞ 1 Complete the table by writing a sentence about, or drawing, what you think could happen next.

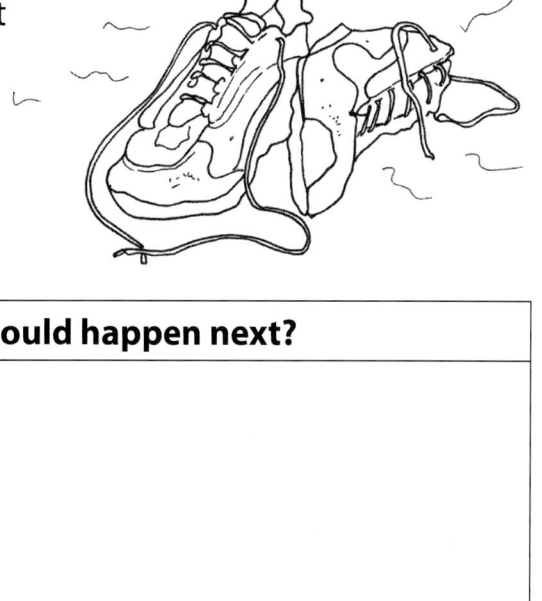

My trainers go…	What could happen next?
In the bin.	
Under my bed.	
To my younger brother.	

Nike's Reuse-A-Shoe programme (www.nikereuseashoe.com) takes old sports shoes and turns them into basketball courts, playgrounds or other Nike products.

☞ 2 Design a trainer collection point for your school where people can place their unwanted trainers for recycling. Remember to include information about:

- Why trainers are being collected
- What recycled trainers can become
- What will happen if unwanted items are not recycled.

© Folens (copiable page)   Sustainable design

Activity sheet – Recycle

Recycle Snap!

Your teacher will provide you with a cut-out copy of the following cards.

☞ 1 Play Recycle Snap! in pairs. Deal the cards face down. Take it in turns to turn over your cards one at a time. If the picture or symbols match, shout Snap! The person who shouts Snap! first wins all of those cards. If the picture that is turned over can be recycled and matches a symbol that is turned over, shout Recycle Snap! The game finishes when one player has won all of the cards.

☞ 2 Play Recycle Pairs. Place the cards face down on a table. Take it in turns to turn over two cards. If they match, that player wins the cards. If they don't match, the cards are turned face down again. The winner is the person with the most matching pairs.

Activity sheet – Recycle

Recycling paper

☞ Create a new papier mâché product.

You will need:

- Plastic sheeting
- Used wrapping paper
- A bucket
- A plastic or metal bowl
- Rubber gloves
- Old newspaper
- PVA glue
- Water
- Wallpaper paste

Step 1

Cover the table with the plastic sheets. Tear the newspaper into strips.

Step 2

Make the wallpaper paste, with water, in the bucket.

Step 3

Soak the strips of newspaper in the wallpaper paste. Remember to wear rubber gloves!

Step 4

Lay the wet paper strips over the outside of the bowl. Make sure you add plenty of layers.

Step 5

Cover the bowl completely and allow the strips to dry.

Step 6

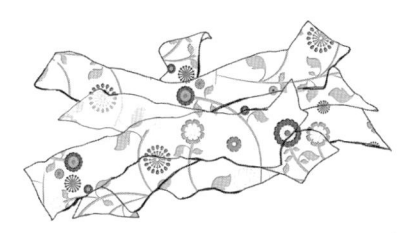

Tear the wrapping paper into strips.

Step 7

Cover the newspaper bowl inside and out with the wrapping paper strips. Use PVA glue to stick the strips to the newspaper bowl.

Allow the strips to dry completely.

You could use your new creation as a fruit bowl!

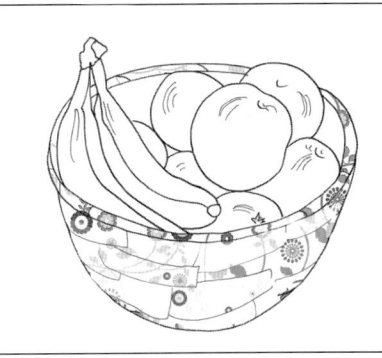

© Folens (copiable page) Sustainable design

Activity sheet – Recycle

Recycled handmade paper

☞ 1 Read about the following items that can be made using handmade paper, created from recycled paper.

☞ 2 Draw another product that can be created using handmade paper. Explain your idea.

A gift tag	**A Christmas card**
Cut a shape out of handmade paper. Use a hole punch or pencil to make a hole in the paper. Thread ribbon, wool or string through the hole to finish your tag.	Use handmade paper to create personalized Christmas cards. You could also create shapes to go on the front of the card.
A bookmark	**Christmas tree decorations**
Cut out a rectangle shape. Create a design and laminate your handmade paper. Punch a hole at the top and thread ribbon, wool or string through to finish your bookmark.	Cut long strips of handmade paper and loop them together. Fix them with glue or sticky tape to create Christmas tree decorations.
Personalized gift bags	**My example**
To jazz up a plain gift bag, cut out handmade paper to create panels to stick on the front.	

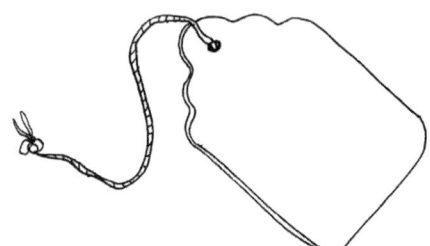

☞ 3 Design and make a useful product using handmade paper.

Sustainable design

Teacher's notes

Reuse

Objectives

- To look at how products can be reused
- To understand how a product's life can be extended beyond its initial use
- To use strategies that promote the reduction of materials
- To try different ways of designing that help to promote a range of ideas

Prior knowledge

Students should be aware that some products can be used more than once.

NC links

Key concepts: 1.1 Designing and making;
1.4 Critical evaluation
Key processes: h
Range and content: c, d, e
Curriculum opportunities: a, b

Northern Ireland PoS

Economic awareness

Scottish attainment targets

Technology: Needs and how they are met: Level C
Resources and how they are managed: Level D

Welsh PoS

Skills: Designing: 2, 4, 8
Skills: Making: 1, 2, 3

Background

The term reuse means to take an existing product that is obsolete or waste and use it or parts of it for another purpose without processing it (processing refers to recycling and turning the material into something else).

In design and technology, products are often reused by either disassembling or reusing its parts for another project.

Starter activity

Students should be encouraged to collect examples of products that have been reused to make other products. Your Tomorrow (www.yourtomorrow.co.uk) is an example of a company that sells products made from reused materials.

Resource sheets and Activity sheets

The following web links could be useful when teaching this unit: the Make-Stuff website provides creative ideas for things to make using waste material (www.make-stuff.com/recycling/index.html); Cardboard Design is an American company that creates items (including furniture) out of recycled cardboard (www.cardboarddesign.com); Recycle Zone is an educational resource about waste and recycling (www.recyclezone.org.uk).

The Activity sheet, 'What can you do with me?', asks students to look at common products that tend to be thrown away or are considered to have little, if any, value. They are required to think of creative uses for each of these products.

The Activity sheet, 'Am I rubbish?', asks students to look at everyday throwaway items as potential children's toys. Students could be encouraged to make an item from the sheet or develop a bigger project, such as using cam wheels on one axle to create an eccentrical moving toy.

The Activity sheet, 'Is it waste?', encourages students to look at how a material can be created using a process that is often done by mistake! Shrinking clothing made out of wool usually means the item is headed for the bin as the fibres become matted and the garment is half its original size. This process is called felting. The felted material can be used to create other items such as a cushion cover.

The Activity sheet, 'Leftover food', asks students to think about what can be done with leftover food by cutting out and spinning the wheel to come up with creative ideas. The Love Food Hate Waste campaign (www.lovefoodhatewaste.com) aims to raise awareness of the need to reduce food waste. Students could also be encouraged to visit Radio 4's *The Food Programme* (www.bbc.co.uk/radio4/factual/foodprogramme_20080106.shtml) for more informaton about leftover food waste.

Students are required to create a hibernation home for insects from waste materials using the Activity sheet, 'Hibernation home'. This is not only a reuse project but an eco-project that aims to create something useful for wildlife.

Plenary

Students could work in groups to identify a range of items and ideas about how they could be reused to create something else.

Activity sheet – Reuse

What can you do with me?

Rather than throwing away or recycling items, they could be reused.

☞ Write down or sketch out two ideas for ways in which each of the following products could be reused. The first one has been done for you.

Product	Idea 1	Idea 2
A plastic carrier bag	Cut into strips and weave them together to create a lining for a pencil case.	Design and make a kite.
Buttons		
Empty plastic containers		
Lolly sticks		
Unwanted CDs		

24   Sustainable design   © Folens (copiable page)

Activity sheet – Reuse

Am I rubbish?

A range of household waste products can be reused to create toys! For example…

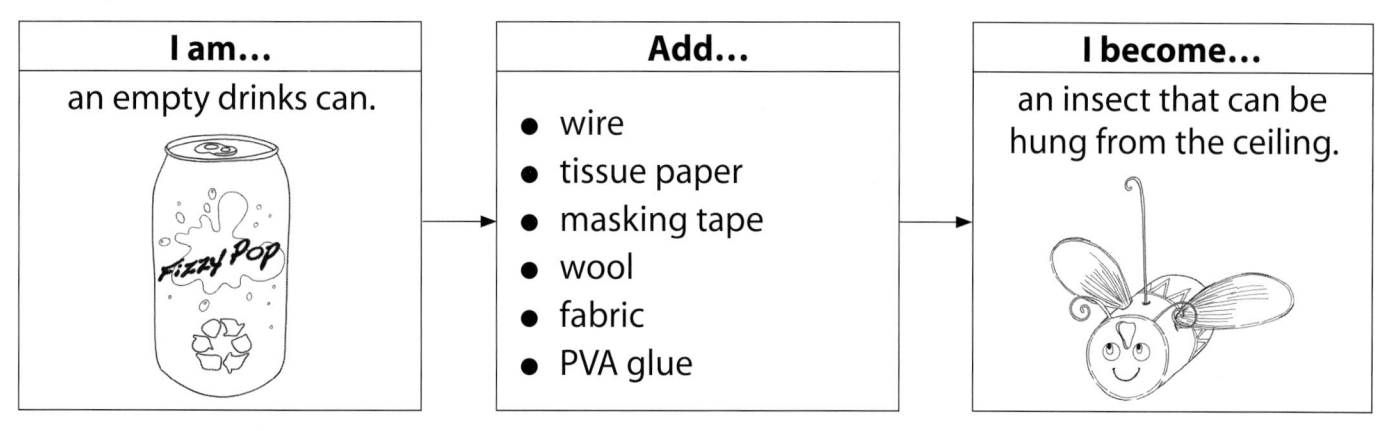

I am…	Add…	I become…
an empty drinks can.	• wire • tissue paper • masking tape • wool • fabric • PVA glue	an insect that can be hung from the ceiling.

☞ 1 Draw what you could make with the following items.

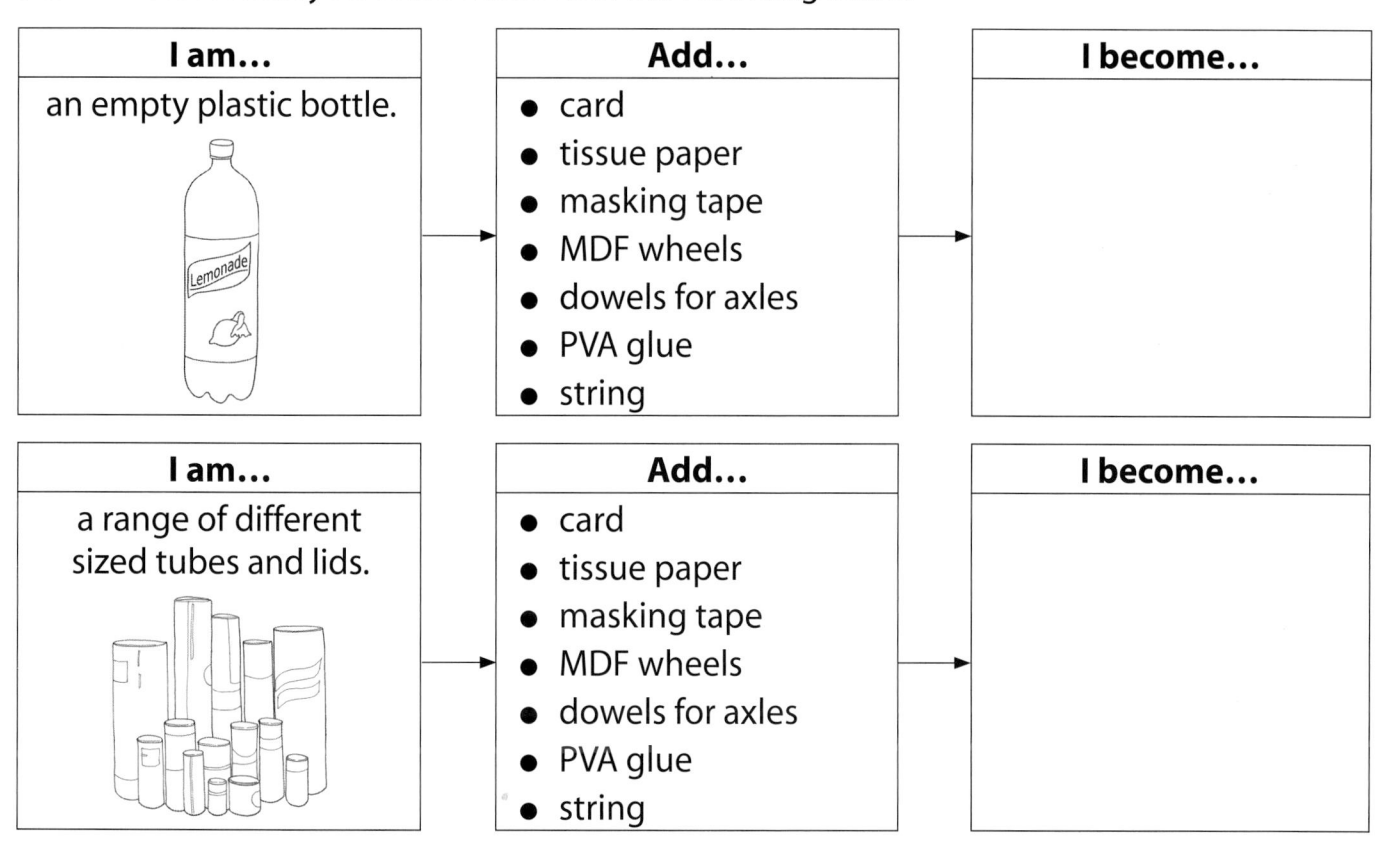

I am…	Add…	I become…
an empty plastic bottle.	• card • tissue paper • masking tape • MDF wheels • dowels for axles • PVA glue • string	

I am…	Add…	I become…
a range of different sized tubes and lids.	• card • tissue paper • masking tape • MDF wheels • dowels for axles • PVA glue • string	

☞ 2 Write down a list of items and draw what you could make with them.

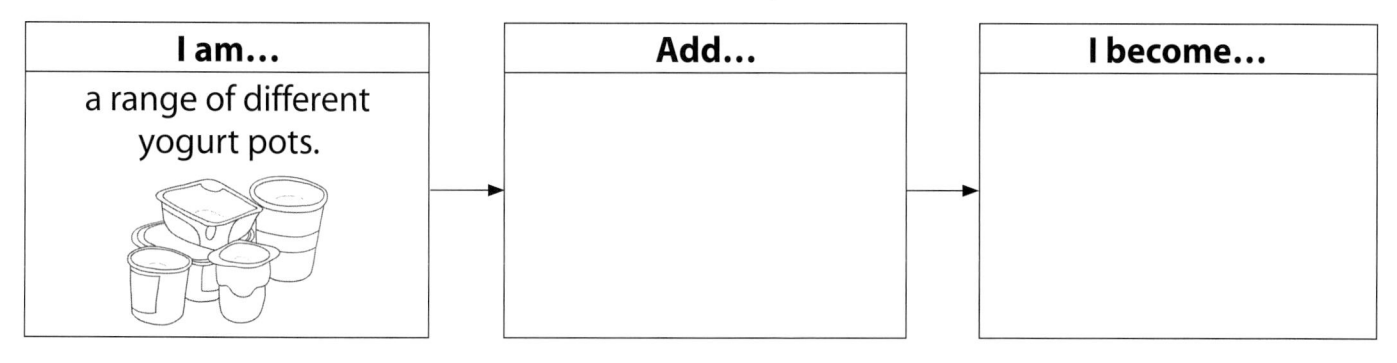

I am…	Add…	I become…
a range of different yogurt pots.		

© Folens (copiable page)   Sustainable design

Activity sheet – Reuse

Is it waste?

How do you make material out of an old woollen garment?

☞ 1 Reuse an old woollen garment by felting it.

You will need:
- An old woollen garment (such as a jumper)
- A sheet of bubble wrap
- Old sheets or towels that will not shrink in a hot wash (make sure they are not dark colours)
- Access to a washing machine
- Laundry soap
- A sewing needle
- Thread

Step 1

Check that the garment you want to felt is discarded and is pure wool (as this will felt better). Remove any buttons, zips or labels.

Step 2

Stitch a sheet of bubble wrap inside the garment to stop its sides felting together.

Step 3

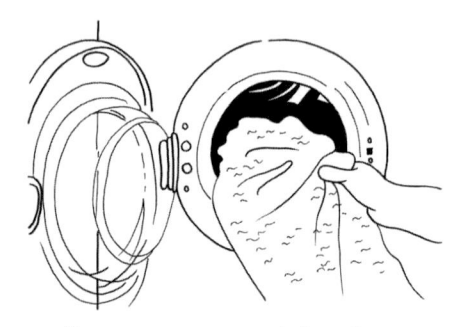

Put the woollen garment and the sheets or towels in the washing machine.

Step 4

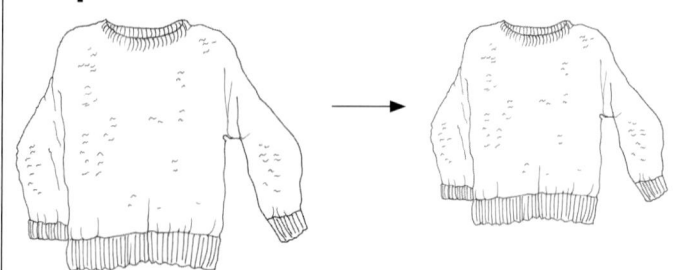

Put the washing on to the hottest wash. The heat will shrink the woollen garment. The fibres will become dense to create felt: a soft, dense fabric.

☞ 2 Once the felt is dry, cut up the fabric and stitch, staple or glue it to create something new such as:

A bag

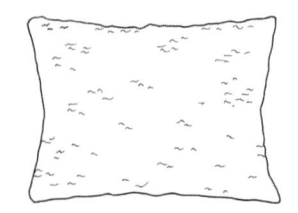

A cushion cover

A piece of jewellery, like a brooch

Activity sheet – Reuse

Leftover food

A third of all food we buy in the UK gets thrown away, even though most of it could be eaten.

☞ 1 Cut out the spin wheel and stick it on to card. Carefully push a pencil through the centre of it.

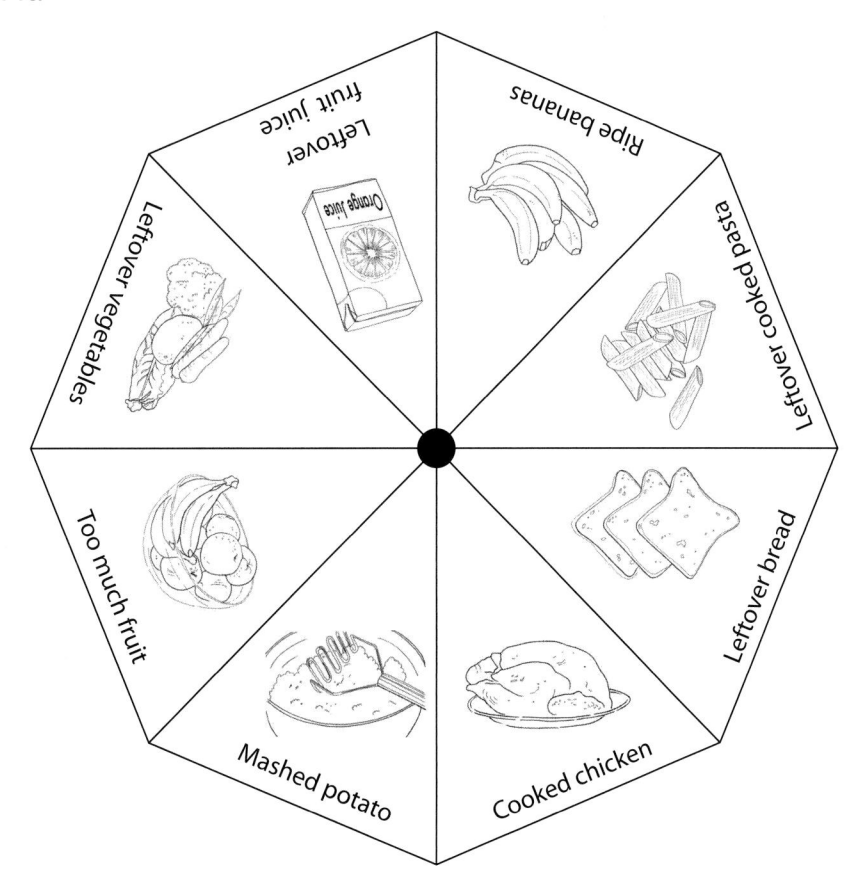

(Spin wheel with eight segments: Leftover fruit juice, Ripe bananas, Leftover cooked pasta, Leftover bread, Cooked chicken, Mashed potato, Too much fruit, Leftover vegetables.)

☞ 2 Cut out the following picture cards.

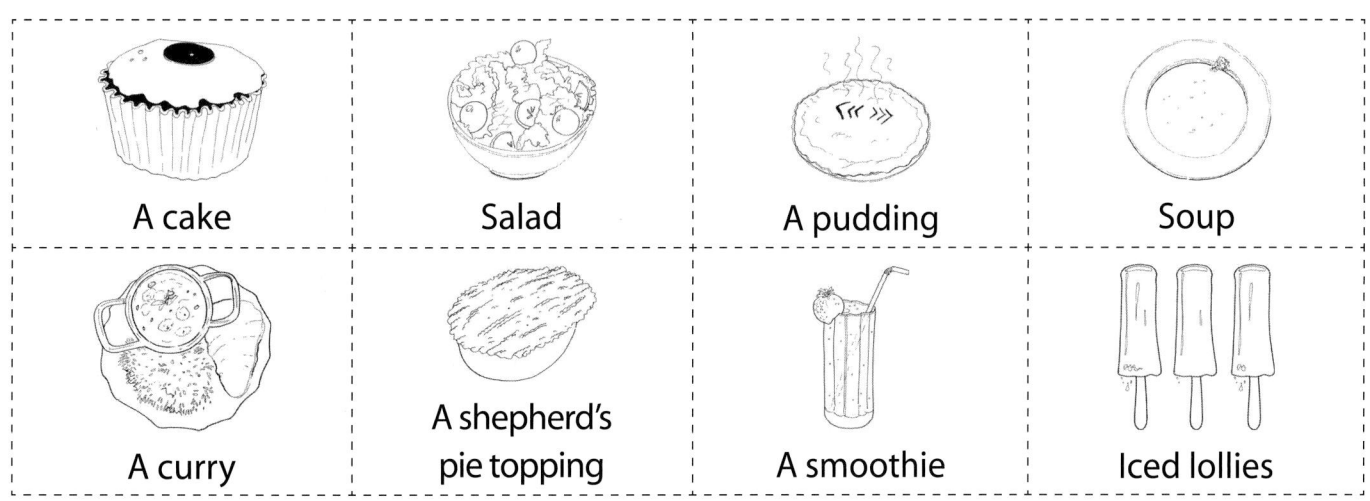

A cake	Salad	A pudding	Soup
A curry	A shepherd's pie topping	A smoothie	Iced lollies

☞ 3 Put the cards face down on the table. Mix them up and choose one. Spin the wheel and think about how you could create a recipe using the items you have chosen!

© Folens (copiable page) Sustainable design

Activity sheet – Reuse

Hibernation home

☞ 1 Create a hibernation home for insects by reusing waste materials. You will need:

- Cardboard tubes with lids and bottoms
- Art straws
- Used A4 paper
- String
- Tissue paper
- Scissors
- PVA glue
- A glue gun
- Gaffer tape
- Corriflute
- A hacksaw

Step 1
Safely use the hacksaw to saw the cardboard tube in half. Use the gaffer tape to secure the lid to the tube.

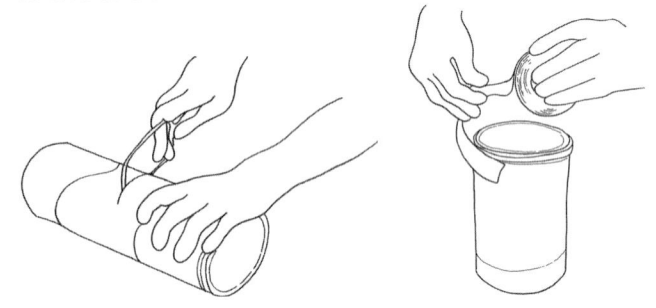

Step 2
Tear up some tissue paper and glue it onto the outside of the tube. Remember to put glue over the tissue paper as well (it will dry to a hard, clear finish and make the tube waterproof).

Step 3
Cut up the art straws and the A4 paper so they are slightly longer than the tube. Roll up the A4 paper into tube shapes. Coat the straws and paper with glue and push them into the tube.

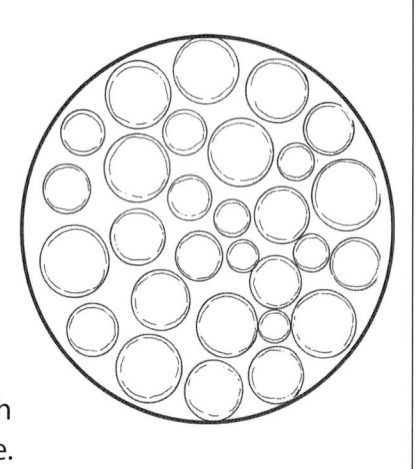

Step 4
Cut out a piece of corriflute measuring 14cm by 10cm. Use scissors to score a line down the centre. This will create the roof of the hibernation home.

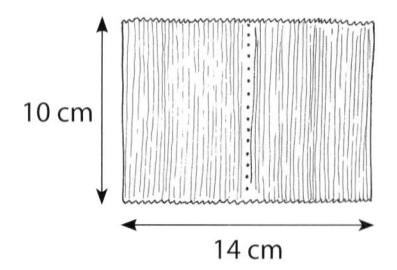

10 cm

14 cm

Step 5
Create a small hole in the centre of the roof. Thread a good length of string through it with a knot at the end. Use the glue gun to fix the roof to the cardboard tube.

Hang your completed hibernation house up outside in the branches of a tree and wait for insects to make their home!

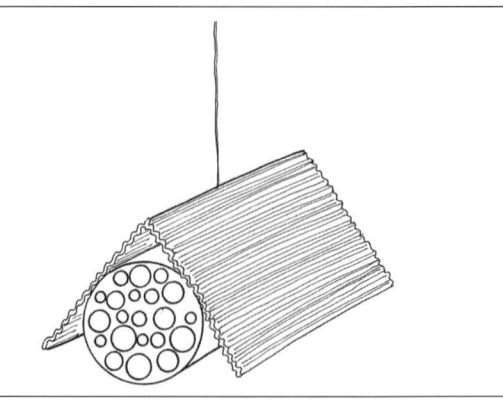

☞ 2 Write down ideas about how you could design and make a bird feeder using a yogurt pot, string, fat and bird seed.

Teacher's notes

Rethink

Objectives

- To understand that products could be manufactured using fewer materials to help reduce the impact they have on the environment
- To learn that by reducing packaging, waste is reduced
- To realize that the product choices we make affect material and fuel usage
- To understand that we should try and source materials from local suppliers

Prior knowledge

Students will have some knowledge of environmental issues and have considered how to reduce their impact on the environment.

NC links

Key concepts: 1.1a, 1.1c Designing and making; 1.2a Cultural understanding
Curriculum opportunities: g

Northern Ireland PoS

Designing: b, e, h
Communicating: a

Scottish attainment targets

Developing informed attitudes – social and environmental responsibility

Welsh PoS

Skills: Designing: 3, 4, 8
Skills: Making: 15

Background

Most students are very aware of the need to recycle as a way of being environmentally friendly, but they also need to be aware of the need to reduce waste at the beginning of a project in order to have a more positive effect on the environment in the long run. This can be done by encouraging students to rethink their work during the initial stages of a project, by considering how products are used, where materials are sourced from and how products are assembled.

Starter activity

Collect, or ask students to collect, a range of product packaging. As a class, discuss how these materials could be reduced at the design stage. Discuss products such as jeans and where the materials come from (for example, cotton for the denim comes from Benin, cotton for the pocketing comes from Pakistan or Korea and copper for the rivets comes from Namibia or Australia).

Resource sheets and Activity sheets

The Resource sheet, 'Ways to rethink', provides students with a range of ideas about how people could rethink their lifestyle and the way products are designed and made. Students could refer back to this sheet throughout the course of the unit.

The Activity sheet, 'Eco-eggs', asks students to consider the possible excessiveness of Easter egg packaging. After looking into the product in detail, students are required to redesign the packaging to rethink the amount of materials used.

The Activity sheet, 'The make-me wheel', asks students to consider a range of products against a number of categories. This is to highlight the range of factors that need to be considered when creating a product. Not all categories are suitable for all products so students should spin the wheel again if necessary.

Students are asked to think about the way they travel to school using the Activity sheet, 'Walk to school campaign'. Based on a class survey, students are to design and create an advertising campaign to encourage more people to rethink the way they travel to school.

Using the Activity sheet, 'Green skateboarding', students are to think about the materials skateboards are made from.

Plenary

As a class, encourage students to discuss how lots of small changes to the way products are created can have a huge impact on the environment. For example, by sourcing materials locally, less fuel is needed to transport them.

Resource sheet – Rethink

Ways to rethink

There are many ways in which we can rethink products to reduce the impact they have on the environment.

- Can it be made so it uses less energy?
- Can it be made from locally sourced materials?
- Can it be manufactured in a different way?
- Can it be made so it can be reused or recycled at the end of its life?
- Can it be made in such a way that it minimizes waste?
- Can it be made from sustainable materials?

For example, an item such as sweetcorn is not just for eating! It can be made into items that are environmentally friendly, such as a bioplastic pen.

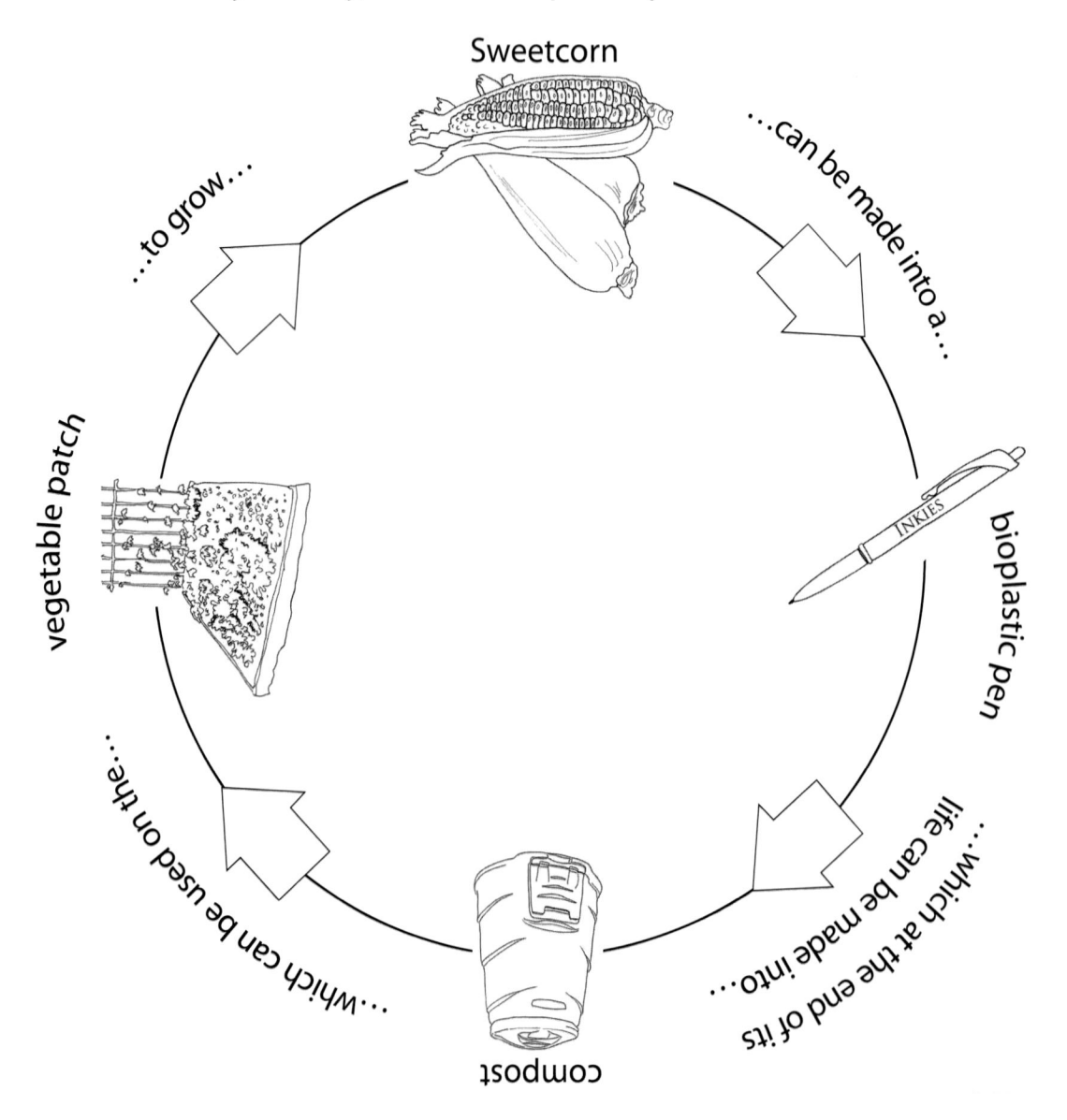

Sweetcorn …can be made into a… bioplastic pen …which at the end of its life can be made into… compost …which can be used on the… vegetable patch …to grow…

Activity sheet – Rethink

Eco-eggs

Easter egg packaging tends to use lots of materials. For example, one Easter egg was 9 per cent chocolate and 91 per cent packaging! Most Easter eggs use three different kinds of packaging: cardboard, plastic and foil.

☞ 1 Take apart an Easter egg's packaging and weigh the materials. Record the weights. Can the materials be recycled?

Easter egg name:		
Material	**Weight**	**Recyclable?**

☞ 2 Write down how you could rethink the packaging of an Easter egg so that fewer materials are used. Design each of the packaging elements of your eco-Easter egg.

© Folens (copiable page)   Sustainable design

Activity sheet – Rethink

The make-me wheel

☞ 1 The wheel below shows different aspects of sustainability. Colour in each of the triangles using a different colour. Cut out the wheel and stick it on to card. Push a pencil through the middle.

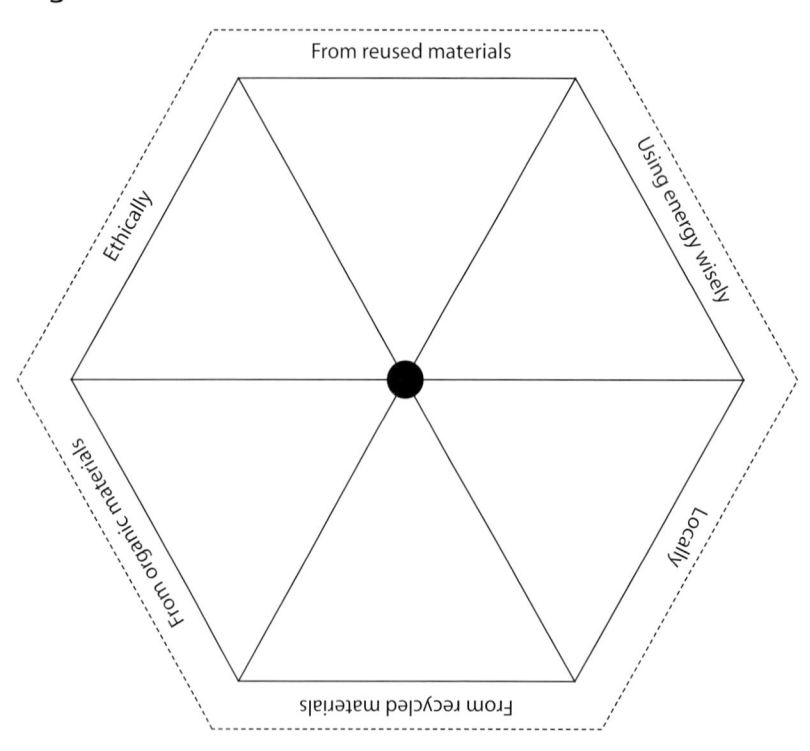

Wheel labels: From reused materials, Using energy wisely, Locally, From recycled materials, From organic materials, Ethically

☞ 2 Spin the wheel to decide which aspect of sustainability you will look at for each of the products below.

☞ 3 Write down which aspect of sustainability you are looking at. Suggest ideas about how the product could be made more sustainably.

Product	Aspect of sustainability	Ideas
A pair of jeans		
A beefburger		
A torch		
A chocolate cake		
A table		

32   Sustainable design   © Folens (copiable page)

Activity sheet – Rethink

Walk to school campaign

☞ 1 Conduct a class survey about how people travel to school. Is the transport type environmentally friendly? Why? Write down what fuel is used, such as 'human power', 'petrol' and so on. Include yourself in the survey.

Type of transport	Number of students	Environmentally friendly?	Fuel used
Bike			
Bus			
Walk			
Car			
Train			
Other			

☞ 2 What can you design and make to encourage more students to use greener ways of travelling to school?

A primary school wants to start a walking bus scheme. The 'bus' is made up of a group of students and two adults. One adult acts as the driver and leads the way, the other acts as a conductor at the back. The group follows a set route, collecting other students on the way.

☞ 3 Design a reflective armband that students taking the walking bus can wear to make them visible.

© Folens (copiable page)   Sustainable design

Activity sheet – Rethink

Green skateboarding

Is your skateboard 'green'? It is made from wood but skateboards can contain harmful compounds such as glues, composites and unsustainably harvested timbers.

The company Comet Skateboards (www.cometskateboards.com) produces socially and environmentally responsible products. They use biodegradable materials, reduce the amount of materials used and source sustainable materials.

☞ 1 Most skateboards are made from plywood. Find out where plywood comes from and how it is used to produce a skateboard.

☞ 2 Why do you think it would be more environmentally friendly to use locally sourced materials to make skateboards?

☞ 3 Design your own eco-friendly skateboard deck using the templates below

Top

Bottom

Teacher's notes

Refuse

Objectives

- To understand what is meant by refuse and how this contributes to sustainability
- To explain what factors might be considered when deciding whether to use a product or not
- To be able to identify how a product could be made more sustainable or to identify a more sustainable alternative for a product

Prior knowledge

Students should be aware that products are designed to meet a need.

NC links

Key concepts: 1.1 Designing and making; 1.4 Critical evaluation
Key processes: h
Range and content: c, d
Curriculum opportunities: a, b

Northern Ireland PoS

Communicating: b
Designing: b

Scottish attainment targets

Technology: Needs and how they are met: Level F; Resources and how they are managed: Level D; Processes and how they are applied: Level D

Welsh PoS

Skills: Designing: 8
Skills: Making: 15

Background

This unit focuses on the choices that we make as consumers and the impact that these choices have on the environment. In particular, it aims to encourage students to refuse to accept products and actions that are unsustainable. The definition of sustainable in this context includes both environmentally friendly materials and processes, and ethical issues such as fair trade, organic products and discouraging the support of child labour.

Starter activity

Using the Internet, students should investigate why child labour was used to produce trainers, a practice first highlighted in the mid-90s. Students should prepare a short verbal presentation on their findings and a select few should be chosen to present to the rest of the class.

Resource sheets and Activity sheets

The Activity sheet, 'Needs and wants', asks students to distinguish between products that are 'needs' or 'wants' so that they can clearly identify the difference between the terms.

The Activity sheet, 'Sustainable alternatives', encourages students to think about sustainable alternatives to a range of products. This aims to highlight that consumers can make choices about the products they buy.

Students are to consider how to make a packaged sandwich more environmentally friendly by completing the task on the Activity sheet, 'Packaged sandwiches'. Students are to investigate ways in which the product's life cycle could be made more sustainable.

The Activity sheet, 'Shoes', asks students to compare trainers with traditional shoes and look at how they could be made by more sustainable methods.

The Activity sheet, 'Ethical trade', requires students to think about ethical decisions when purchasing products. Students are to consider the advantages and disadvantages of buying from two different farms and make a decision about which farm they would buy from, based on their own judgement.

Plenary

In small groups, students are to study a number of different products. They should decide what issues relating to the product would cause them to refuse to buy it. For the products that are refused, students should come up with ways to make them more sustainable so they would buy them.

Activity sheet – Refuse

Needs and wants

Needs are things that are important to our life. For example, we <u>need</u> water and food in order to live.

Wants are things that are usually luxury items, things that we could live without. For example, although we need water in order to live, we <u>want</u> fizzy drinks because they taste nice. Items that are wants can make our lives more comfortable.

☞ 1 Study the items listed below. List the items you think are needs, wants or neither.

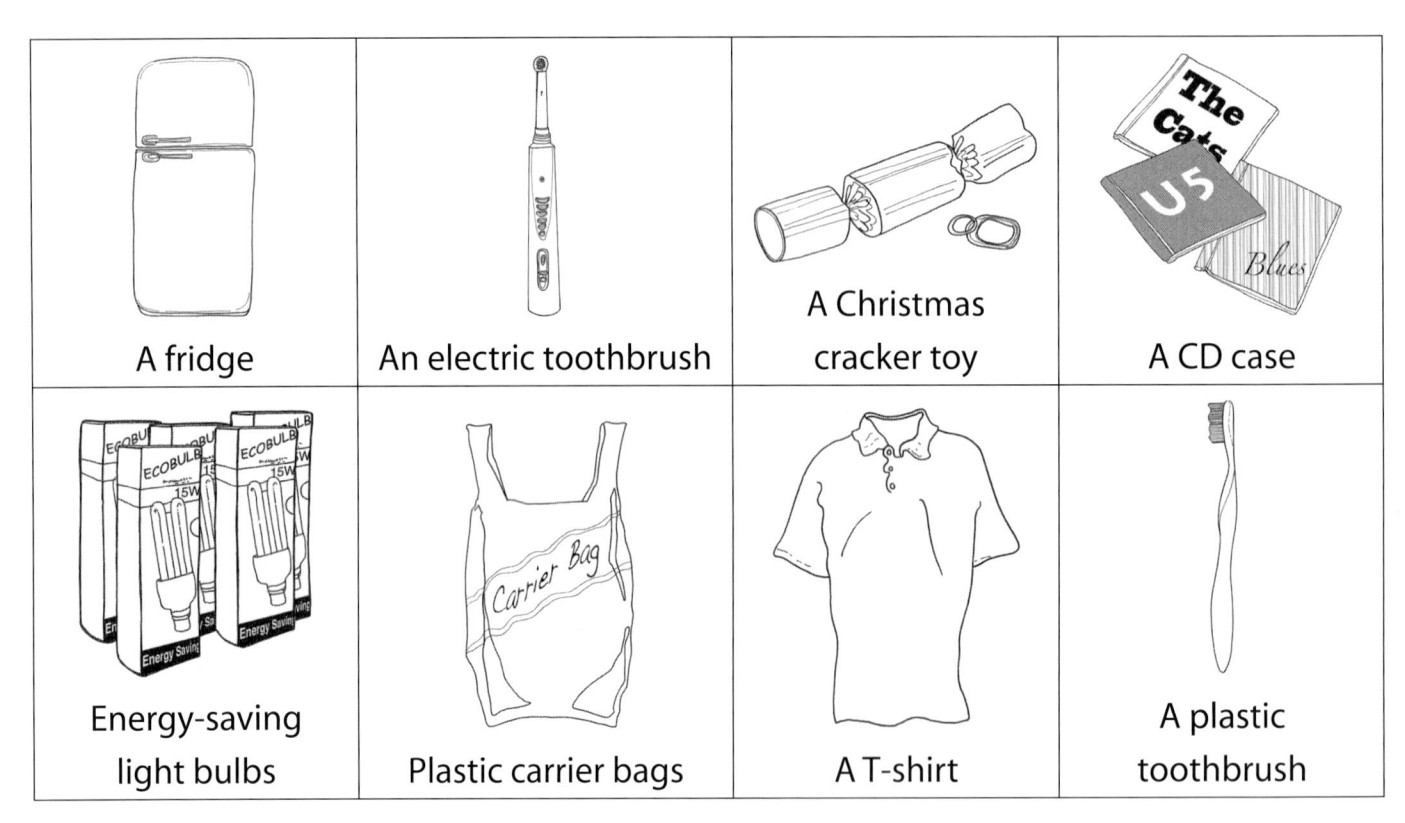

| A fridge | An electric toothbrush | A Christmas cracker toy | A CD case |
| Energy-saving light bulbs | Plastic carrier bags | A T-shirt | A plastic toothbrush |

Needs	Wants	Neither

☞ 2 Add two more of your own examples to each column.

36   Sustainable design   © Folens (copiable page)

Activity sheet – Refuse

Sustainable alternatives

Something that is sustainable means that it can easily be replaced, without using up natural resources.

Consumers often have a choice about what products they buy. Before buying a product, check if there is a more sustainable version available.

☞ Link the items on the left with a more sustainable version by drawing an arrow between them. An example has been done for you.

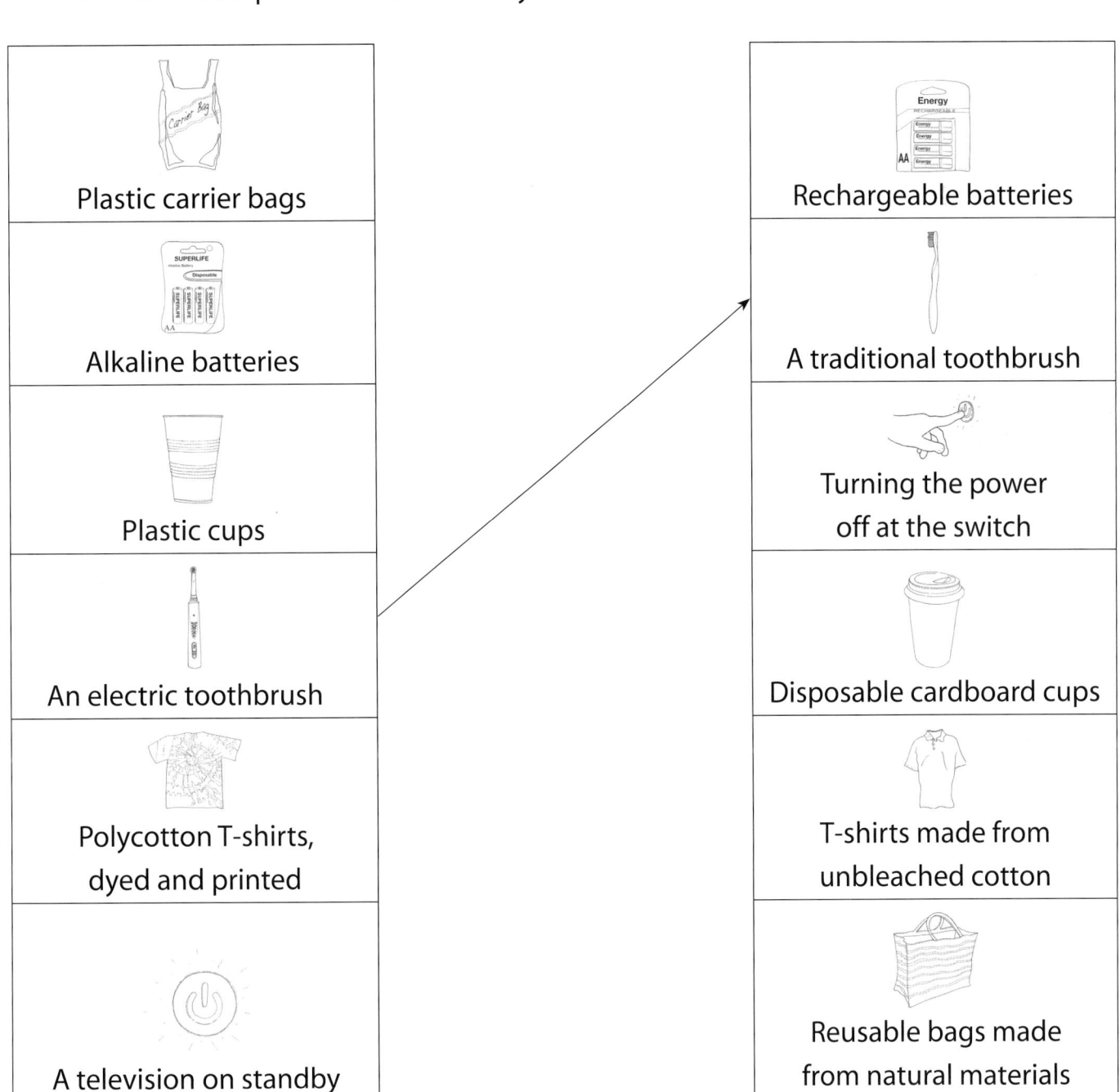

Plastic carrier bags	Rechargeable batteries
Alkaline batteries	A traditional toothbrush
Plastic cups	Turning the power off at the switch
An electric toothbrush	Disposable cardboard cups
Polycotton T-shirts, dyed and printed	T-shirts made from unbleached cotton
A television on standby	Reusable bags made from natural materials

© Folens (copiable page)   Sustainable design   37

Activity sheet – Refuse

Packaged sandwiches

Packaged sandwiches are a convenience food. A typical packaged cheese and tomato sandwich may contain:

- Bread with additives and preservatives to stop it going stale
- Cheese that contains genetically engineered rennet (an ingredient used to help milk turn into cheese)
- Tomatoes grown outside the UK.

The sandwich below is packaged in plastic and sealed with plastic film. It was made in a small factory 30 miles from the shop that sells it. It was transported in a cardboard box by a refrigerated van.

☞ 1 Add comments below to explain how the life cycle of this sandwich could be improved to make it more environmentally friendly.

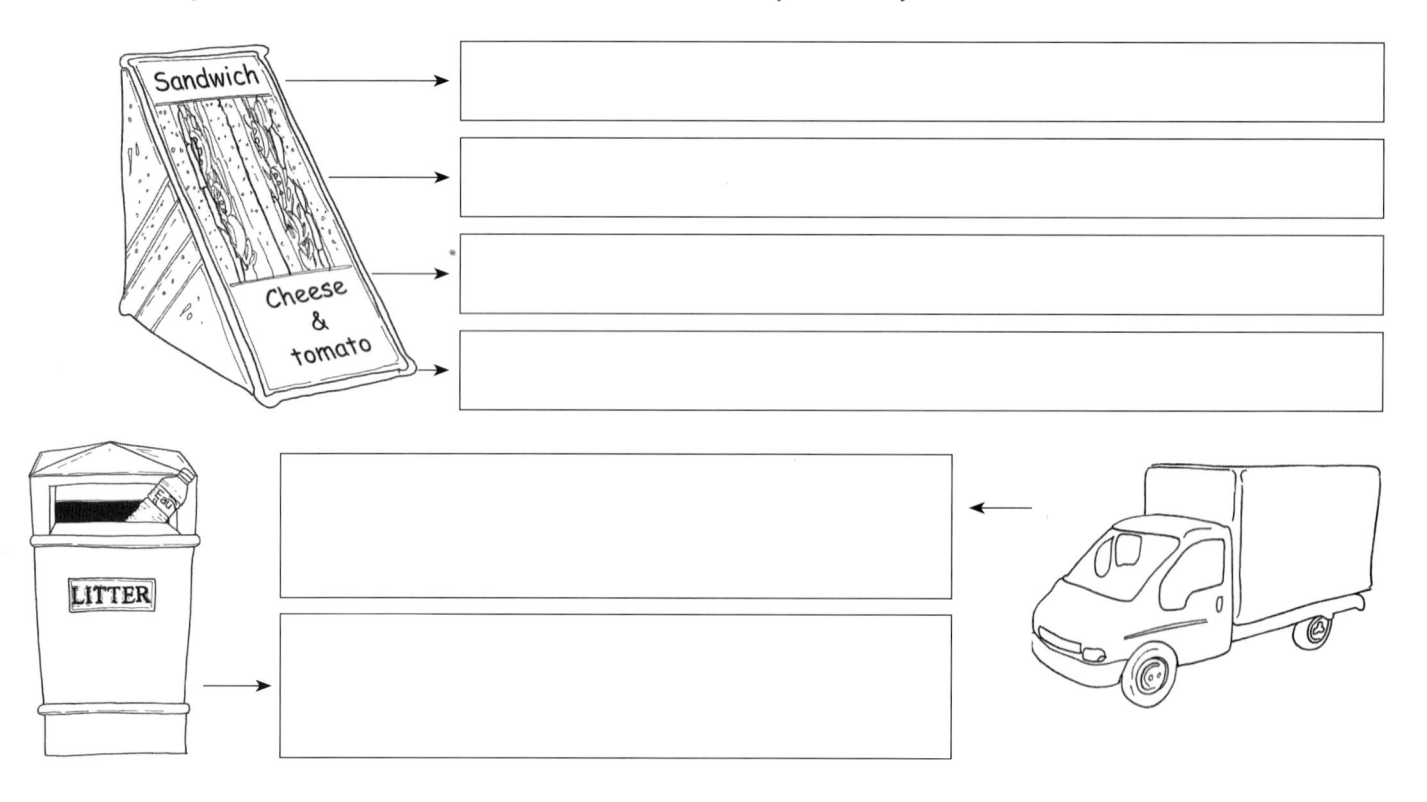

☞ 2 Explain how your proposed changes will affect the cost of the sandwich.

___

___

___

38   Sustainable design   © Folens (copiable page)

Activity sheet – Refuse

Shoes

Although trainers are mainly designed to be worn when playing sports, lots of people wear them as a fashion item. They can contain lots of different materials so they can bend and cushion the foot on impact. Look at the label to find out where your trainers were made.

Traditional shoes are usually made of leather or plastic, with a leather, rubber or plastic sole. Look at the label to find out where your shoes were made.

Trainers

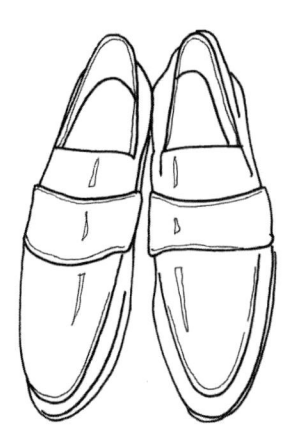

Traditional shoes

☞ Compare trainers and shoes. In the space below, decide which one you think is the most sustainable. Use words from the ideas bank to help you.

The _____ are the most sustainable because

_____

_____

_____

_____

_____

Ideas bank
• Local   • Fair wage   • Materials   • Renewable sources

© Folens (copiable page)   Sustainable design   39

Activity sheet – Refuse

Ethical trade

Making ethical choices about which products you buy means making decisions about different factors.

A drinks company wants to buy fruit from one of two farms in South America to make a juice drink. It will cost them the same amount to buy fruit from either farm.

- Farm A uses pesticides to stop insects eating the fruit. The fruit is picked by children. They are paid 50p a day.
- Farm B does not use pesticides on their fruit. The farm is not always able to supply fruit because the insects eat it. The fruit is picked by adults. They are paid up to £5 per day.

☞ 1 Complete the table with the advantages and disadvantages for the drinks company of buying fruit from either farm.

a) Fruit is always available to buy
b) No pesticides are used
c) Cheap child labour is used
d) Fruit is not always available to buy
e) More expensive adult labour is used
f) Pesticides are used

	Advantages	Disadvantages
Farm A		
Farm B		

☞ 2 Which farm do you think the drinks company should buy their fruit from? Why?

_____
_____
_____

Teacher's notes

Fair trade

Objectives

- To understand what the term 'fair trade' means
- To learn about the Fairtrade Foundation and what the FAIRTRADE Mark means
- To realize that consumer's product choices can greatly affect the lives of others

Prior knowledge

Students should understand that products are made and sold for profit. They should understand that obtaining a fair wage is important for people's livelihoods and that people work to earn money to pay for goods and services.

NC links

Key concepts: 1.1a, 1.1c Designing and making; 1.2a Cultural understanding
Curriculum opportunities: g

Northern Ireland PoS

Designing: b, e, h
Communicating: a

Scottish attainment targets

Strands and targets in environmental studies: developing informed attitudes

Welsh PoS

Skills: Designing: 3, 4, 8
Skills: Making: 15

Background

Fair trade is about achieving better prices for products, decent working conditions, local sustainability and fair terms of trade for farmers and workers in the developing world. The Fairtrade Foundation (www.fairtrade.org.uk) is an independent, non-profit organization that licenses the use of the FAIRTRADE Mark on products in the UK in accordance with internationally agreed Fairtrade standards. The Foundation aims to eradicate injustices of conventional trade, which traditionally discriminates against poorer and disadvantaged producers, by enabling them to improve their trading position, giving them more control over their lives.

Starter activity

Students should be provided with a range of examples of fair trade goods (those with the FAIRTRADE Mark) to promote a class discussion about where the items have come from and who might have produced them.

Resource sheets and Activity sheets

The Resource sheet, 'What is fair trade?', introduces students to what fair trade is and to the non-profit organization, the Fairtrade Foundation. Students can refer back to the sheet during the course of the unit in order to consider fair trade activities.

Students are encouraged to use an atlas and the Internet to find out which countries products come from using the Activity sheet, 'Where in the world?'. This will help them to visualize how far products have to travel in order to be sold in the UK. Potential answers include (but are not limited to) bananas from India, Brazil, China and the Windward Islands; cotton from India, China, the United States and Egypt; cocoa beans are the seed of a tree indigenous to the equatorial regions of the Americas; tea from China and Kenya; and honey from Mexico, Australia and the UK.

The Activity sheet, 'That's not fair!', asks students to look at the growing and transportation of bananas and who makes most of the profit. By completing this activity students will have a better idea of the conflict of interests between those that deal in this product.

Students are encouraged to look at the promotion of Fairtrade coffee using the Activity sheet, 'A lovely cup of coffee'. This activity will highlight the importance of advertising Fairtrade products to help improve sales of these items, improving the lives of poorer suppliers.

The Activity sheet, 'Chocolate heaven', requires students to design a new chocolate bar that would meet the Fairtrade Foundation's standards to achieve the FAIRTRADE Mark. Students could be encouraged to visit websites of companies that make fair trade chocolate such as Divine Chocolate www.divinechocolate.com and Dubble www.dubble.co.uk.

Plenary

Ask students to explain why buying Fairtrade products makes a difference to the producers. Students could be encouraged to carry out further research by using the websites provided on this page. Students could organize activities in school for the annual Fairtrade Fortnight campaign or campaign to become a Fairtrade school (www.fairtrade.org.uk/schools/default.aspx).

Resource sheet – Fair trade

What is fair trade?

Fair trade is about helping farmers and workers in the developing world to achieve better prices for products and decent working conditions.

The Fairtrade Foundation is a non-profit organization that aims to improve the lives of poorer and disadvantaged producers from developing countries. It enables them to improve their trading position and gives them more control over their lives.

The Fairtrade Foundation licenses the use of the FAIRTRADE Mark on products in the UK.

Have you seen the FAIRTRADE Mark on these products?

Activity sheet – Fair trade

Where in the world?

☞ 1 Use an atlas and the Internet to find out which countries the following products come from. Remember, these products can come from more than one country.

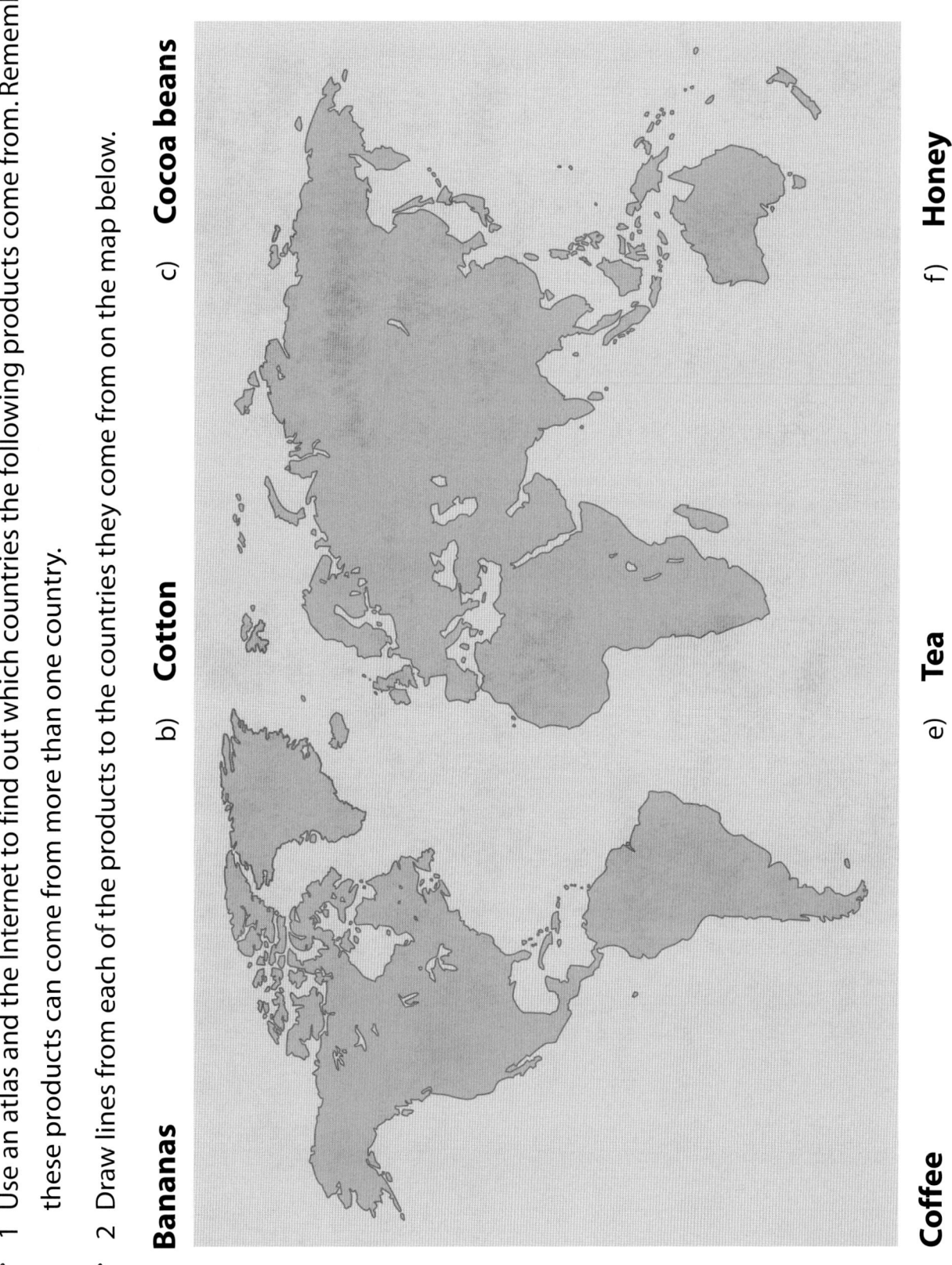

☞ 2 Draw lines from each of the products to the countries they come from on the map below.

a) **Bananas**   b) **Cotton**   c) **Cocoa beans**

d) **Coffee**   e) **Tea**   f) **Honey**

© Folens (copiable page)   Sustainable design   43

Activity sheet – Fair trade

That's not fair!

Imagine you work for a banana farm in India. Everyone in the supply chain gets a percentage of the total cost of the bananas that the farm produces. Even if the bananas do not sell, everyone in the chain still has to be paid.

- The supermarkets that sell the bananas get **45 per cent**
- The company that imported and ripened the bananas gets **18 per cent**
- The transporter that exported the bananas gets **19 per cent**
- The banana farm (the producer) that grew the bananas gets **15.5 per cent**
- The workers on the banana farm get **2.5 per cent**

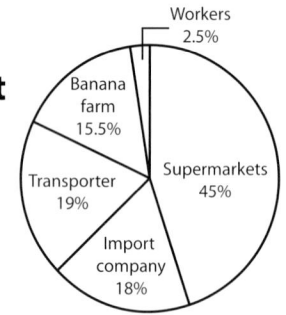

☞ 1 Think about each of the suppliers and imagine what it must be like to be them.

☞ 2 Write down what you think each of the suppliers want from the banana trade. An example has been given to help you.

Supermarkets	Import company
Good quality products at a rock-bottom price to sell for a large profit.	
Transporter	**Banana farm**
Workers	

☞ 3 How do you think the banana trade would be affected by fair trade? Do you think it makes things better for everyone in the supply chain?

Sustainable design

Activity sheet – Fair trade

A lovely cup of coffee

A local coffee shop has been selling Fairtrade coffee to its customers for a long time, but they do not advertise it in any way.

☞ 1 Create a mug design to let customers know about the product they are drinking. Use the templates below to help plan your design.

Front   Back

The coffee shop would also like to reward loyal customers with a free cup of coffee.

☞ 2 Design a loyalty card that customers can get stamped every time they buy a Fairtrade coffee. When they have collected nine stamps, they can get their tenth coffee for free.

Black Coffee

Have your 10th coffee absolutely free!

© Folens (copiable page)　　Sustainable design　　45

Activity sheet – Fair trade

Chocolate heaven

Millions of chocolate bars are sold every day, but cocoa farmers are some of the poorest people in the world. They earn about 50p per kilo of cocoa. Most cocoa farmers can't demand a higher price for their cocoa because they depend on selling their products in order to live.

You have been asked to design a chocolate bar wrapper for a new Fairtrade product called 'Heavenly'.

☞ 1 Use the space below to design the font you will use on the chocolate bar wrapper.

☞ 2 Use the net below to design the chocolate bar wrapper. Remember, the middle section will be the front of the wrapper. The other two sections will be wrapped around the back of the bar.

Teacher's notes

Renewable energy

Objectives

- To understand what is meant by the term 'renewable energy source'
- To explain how wind power is used to generate electricity
- To explain how solar power is used to generate electricity
- To describe a range of approaches to reduce the usage of unsustainable energy requirements, either through reducing energy needs or implementing renewable energy sources

Prior knowledge

Students should be aware of electricity and the function of an electric dynamo.

NC links

Key concepts: 1.1 Designing and making; 1.4 Critical evaluation
Key processes: h
Range and content: c, d, e
Curriculum opportunities: a, b

Northern Ireland PoS

Designing: b
Using energy and control: b

Scottish attainment targets

Technology: Needs and how they are met: Level D
Resources and how they are managed: Level E
Processes and how they are applied: Level D
Science: Conversion and transfer of energy: Level C

Welsh PoS

Skills: Designing: 8

Background

This unit introduces the idea of renewable sources of energy. It aims to encourage students to consider how they are using electricity, where that energy comes from and how the requirement for non-renewable energy can be reduced.

Starter activity

In small groups, students should write down a list of all the different types of electrical equipment that they have used in the last week. The aim of this activity is to highlight the extent to which modern life is dependant upon energy. To extend this activity, students could be encouraged to provide ideas as to what they could do if energy wasn't available, for example, use a candle instead of a light bulb, read a book instead of watching television, and so on.

Resource sheets and Activity sheets

The Resource sheet, 'Electricity', provides students with a range of sources of energy. This can be referred to during the completion of the unit.

The Activity sheet, 'What is renewable energy?', outlines to students the differences between renewable and non-renewable energy. Students are required to apply their knowledge of these terms to categorize different types of energy.

The Activity sheet, 'Wind power', encourages students to think about other ways in which electricity can be generated.

The Activity sheet, 'Solar power', requires students to consider the pros and cons of solar power and to think about ways in which solar power can be used.

Students are required to apply their knowledge of renewable energy in order to come up with viable solutions to create an eco-friendly home using the Activity sheet, 'Eco-friendly homes'. An important feature of reducing dependence on non-renewable resources is to reduce the need for energy. Students are asked to consider this when completing the activity.

Plenary

In small groups, students should prepare a presentation to a company that designs new homes, explaining how they could make the homes environmentally friendly.

Resource sheet – Renewable energy
Electricity

Electricity is a type of energy. There are lots of different ways to generate electricity.

Most of our electricity is generated using oil and gas. Oil and gases are obtained by drilling deep into the ground.	Wind turbines use energy from the wind to generate electricity.
Solar panels use energy from sunlight to generate electricity.	Deep underground the rocks are hot. We can use the heat energy to generate electricity.
The energy from the tides of the sea can be used to generate electricity.	The heat from radioactive materials (thermonuclear) can be used to generate electricity.

Sustainable design

Activity sheet – Renewable energy

What is renewable energy?

Electricity is often generated by burning some form of fuel. The fuel is used up and destroyed as electricity is generated. It can take millions of years for new fuel to form to replace all of the fuel that is used. This means it could run out.

A non-renewable energy source is something that is not easily replaced or could run out altogether.

Renewable energy is energy that is made from something that can easily be replaced.

☞ Match the following words with their description. Decide if the energy source is renewable or not. An example has been given to help you.

- ~~Nuclear power~~
- Solar power
- Oil
- Tidal power
- Wind power
- Geothermal power
- Gas

How energy is generated	Energy source	Is it renewable?
Heat from radioactive materials	Nuclear power	Yes / ~~No~~
Heat from deep underground		Yes / No
By using petrol		Yes / No
From sunlight		Yes / No
Found by drilling into the ground and burning it to make energy		Yes / No
From moving air		Yes / No
From waves in the sea		Yes / No

© Folens (copiable page)   Sustainable design

Activity sheet – Renewable energy

Wind power

You may have a dynamo on your bike. When you pedal your bike it generates electricity for your light. Wind can be used to generate electricity by using a wind turbine.

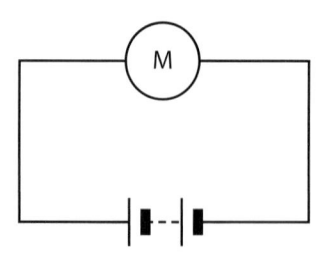

☞ 1 Complete the following paragraph about how wind turbines work by using the words listed.

- electricity
- wind
- generator

The _____ turns the blades of the propeller. The propeller is connected to a gearbox which turns a _____ . This generates _____ .

☞ 2 Label parts of a wind turbine using the following words:

- Propeller
- Gearbox and generator
- Support

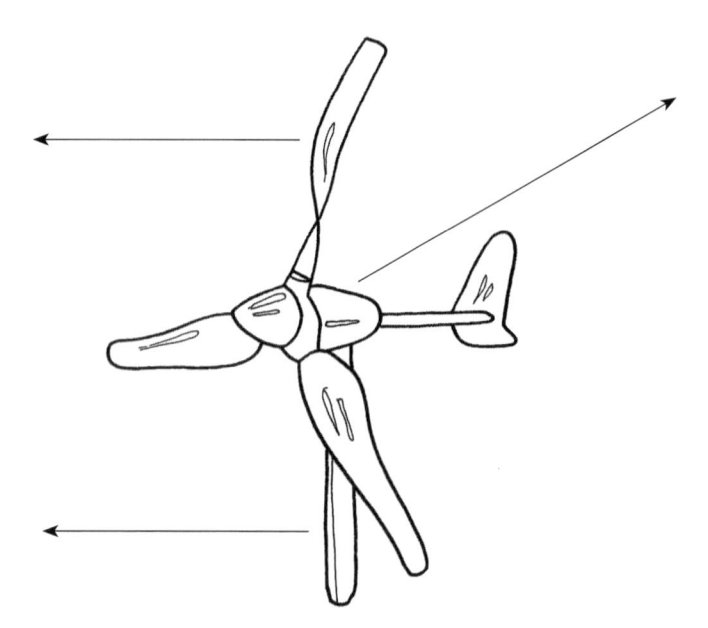

However, when there is no wind the wind turbine propellers won't turn. This means electricity can't be generated.

☞ 3 Explain what could be done to generate electricity when there is no wind.

_____

_____

_____

50   Sustainable design   © Folens (copiable page)

Activity sheet – Renewable energy

Solar power

Solar panels use energy from sunlight to generate electricity. If it is cloudy or night-time, sufficient electricity cannot be generated.

☞ 1 Complete the table by writing the following items in the correct column to say whether solar energy could be used to make them work. An example has been given to help you.

- ~~Street lighting~~
- Cooling fans
- Electric-powered ambulances
- School lights and equipment
- Heating
- Calculators

Solar energy could be used for…	Solar energy couldn't be used for…
	Street lighting

☞ 2 Solar panels only generate electricity when it is sunny. Explain what could be done to make sure that electricity is available when you need it at night. Use the ideas box to help you.

_____

_____

Ideas box
• Power   • Energy   • Electricity   • Solar   • Cell   • Panel

Activity sheet – Renewable energy

Eco-friendly homes

There are two ways that can help to reduce the amount of non-renewable energy that is used in the home:

1. Reduce the amount of products you use that need energy.
2. Use more renewable energy sources.

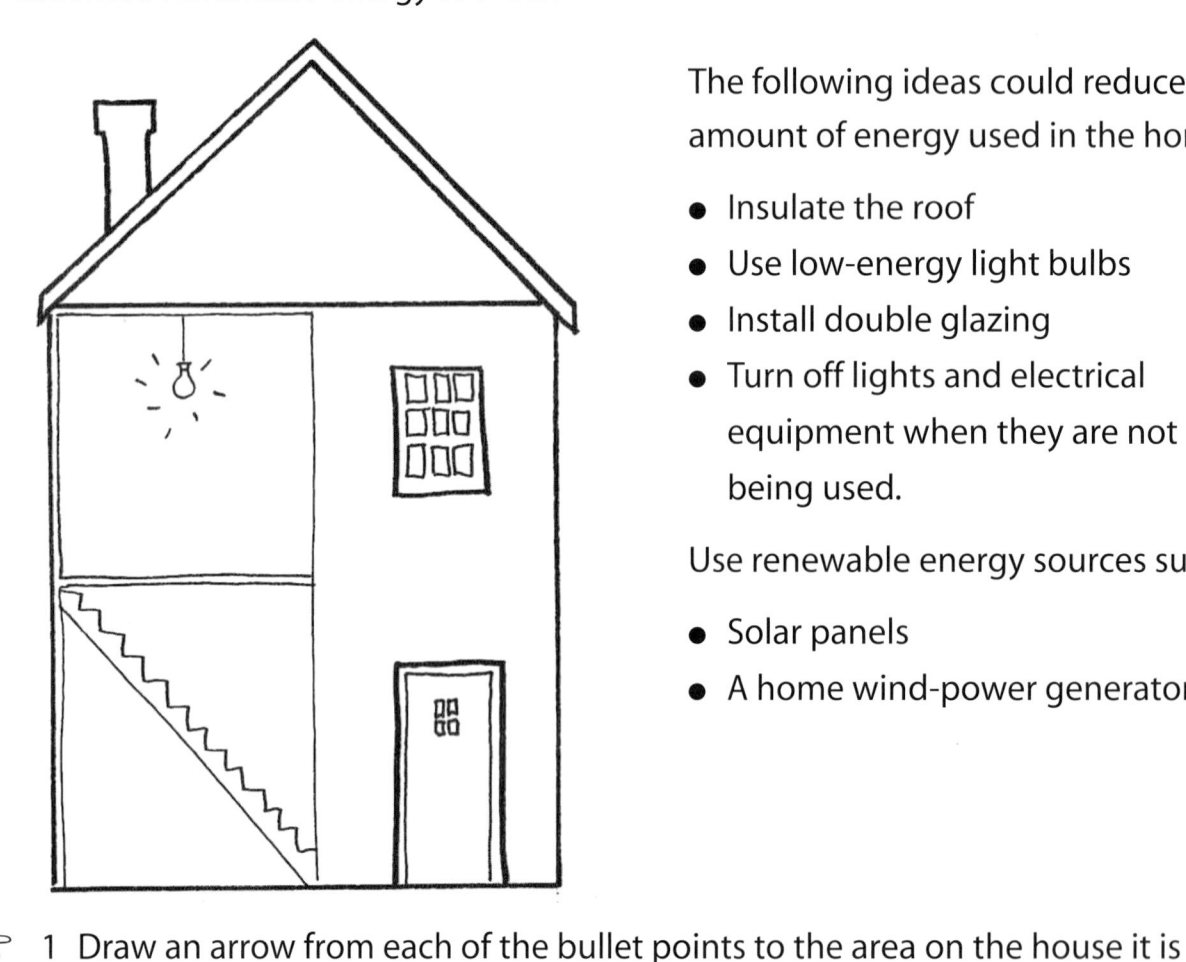

The following ideas could reduce the amount of energy used in the home:

- Insulate the roof
- Use low-energy light bulbs
- Install double glazing
- Turn off lights and electrical equipment when they are not being used.

Use renewable energy sources such as:

- Solar panels
- A home wind-power generator.

☞ 1 Draw an arrow from each of the bullet points to the area on the house it is referring to. Or add a sketch to the house showing how it could be applied.

☞ 2 Write about two other things that you could do at home to save electricity.

_____
_____
_____
_____
_____

Teacher's notes

Alternative choices

Objectives
- To understand that making choices can have an impact on the way we use resources
- To investigate alternative ideas that could be more sustainable
- To use strategies that promote sustainability

Prior knowledge
Students need to have an understanding of the meaning of the 6Rs and appreciate that everyone has a responsibility for the choices that they make in their life.

NC links
Key concepts: 1.1 Designing and making; 1.4 Critical evaluation
Key processes: h
Range and content: c, d, e
Curriculum opportunities: a, b

Northern Ireland PoS
Using energy and control

Scottish attainment targets
Technology: Needs and how they are met: Level C
Resources and how they are managed: Level D

Welsh PoS
Skills: Designing: 2, 4, 8
Skills: Making: 1, 2, 3

Starter activity
The Resource sheet, 'Alternative choices', covers some of the 6Rs, providing examples of how they can be used to create a cushion. Ask students to recreate the table from this Resource sheet and fill it in for a product of their choosing.

Resource sheets and Activity sheets
The Activity sheet, 'Material choices', requires students to think about different material choices they can make to create a variety of products. This aims to highlight to students that there are a wide range of alternative materials that can be used when designing products.

The Activity sheet, 'Transport choices', asks students to look closely at transport choices and how they affect the environment. Students are required to rank the choices but this could be extended to a class discussion. They should consider the cost (petrol and parking charges for example) and time issues of different transport.

The Activity sheet, 'Build a land yacht', is a hands-on project for students to have fun with. They are required to create a land yacht that uses the power of wind to make it move. Students could race their final products against each other or measure the distance their wind yacht travels with one puff of wind. This task could be extended by using solar panels to drive a motor.

Plenary
Students could create a stick-it note challenge poster entitled 'Change one thing'. Students should write down on a stick-it note one small change they could make to reduce their impact on the environment and display it on the poster. After a week, students should tick their stick-it note if they were successful in fulfilling their promise.

Background

This unit looks at how we can do our bit to preserve the earth's valuable resources by identifying ways in which resources can be reused, and highlighting alternative choices that people can make to reduce the amount of resources they use.

The company [re]design (www.redesigndesign.org) run workshops, give lectures and put on exhibitions about designing products sustainably. Another resource about sustainable design is *The Eco-design Handbook* by Alastair Fuad-Luke. This book outlines green design strategies and material sources to create objects for the home and office.

Resource sheet – Alternative choices

Alternative choices

You should decide on the materials for a project at the very start. This is why it is important to research what materials you can use as early as possible.

For example, if you were designing a cushion cover, you could make the following choices using one, or some, of the 6Rs:

Materials required	Choices that could be made
1 Fabric	Reuse unwanted clothing to create a patchwork for the cushion cover.
2 Felt for the pattern	Reuse an old woollen garment to create felt.
3 Ribbon for decoration	Reuse unwanted clothing to create ribbon by cutting strips of material with pinking shears.
4 A zip	Reuse a zip from an unwanted item of clothing.
5 Thread	Reuse long pieces of cotton, wool or string.
6 Beads and buttons for decoration	Reuse beads and buttons from unwanted items of clothing.

When choosing materials it is important that they are of a good quality. The following items are all things that can be reused in new projects. However, you need to make sure that they work and are of a good quality.

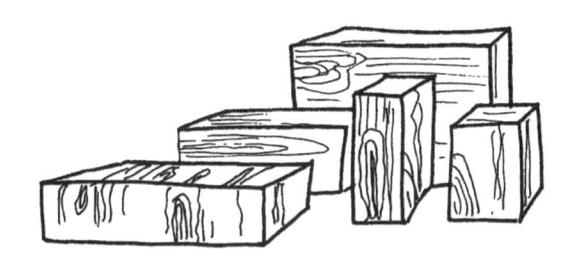

Wood offcuts

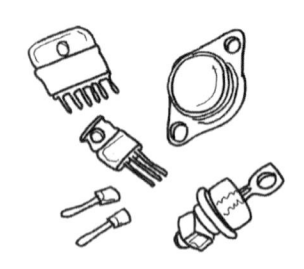

Electronic components

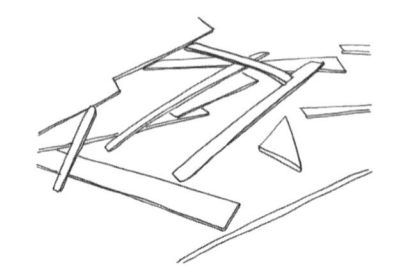

Waste from a vacuum-formed product

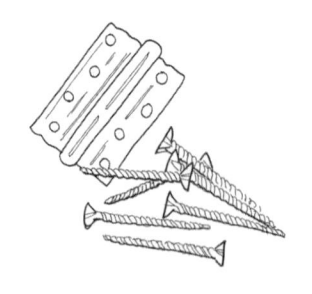

Hinges and screws.

54 Sustainable design © Folens (copiable page)

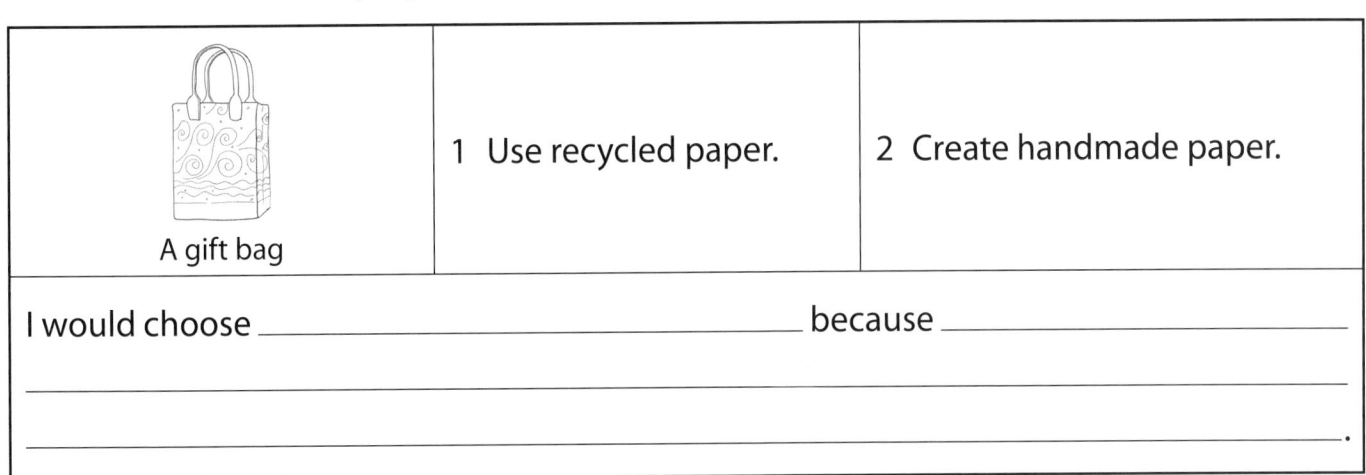

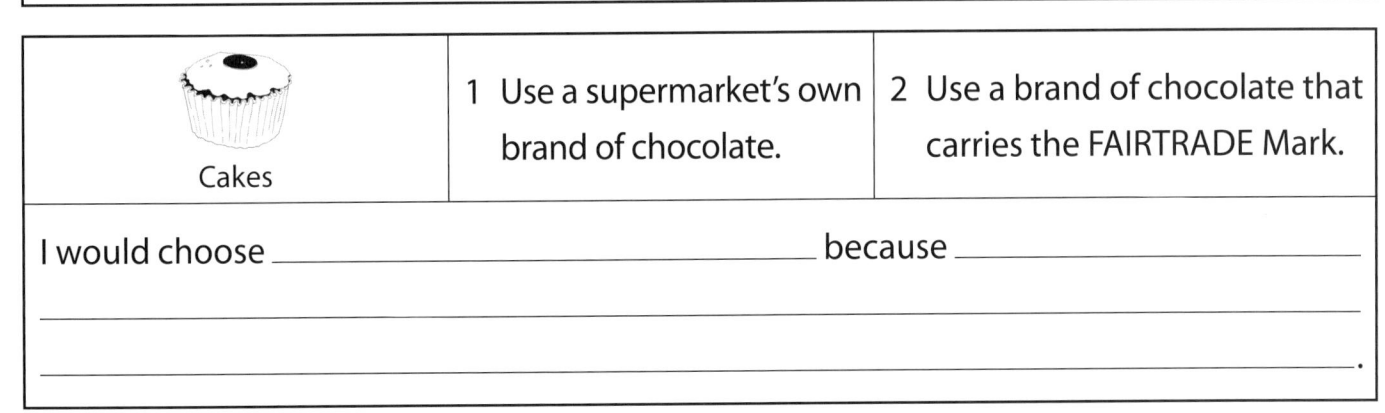

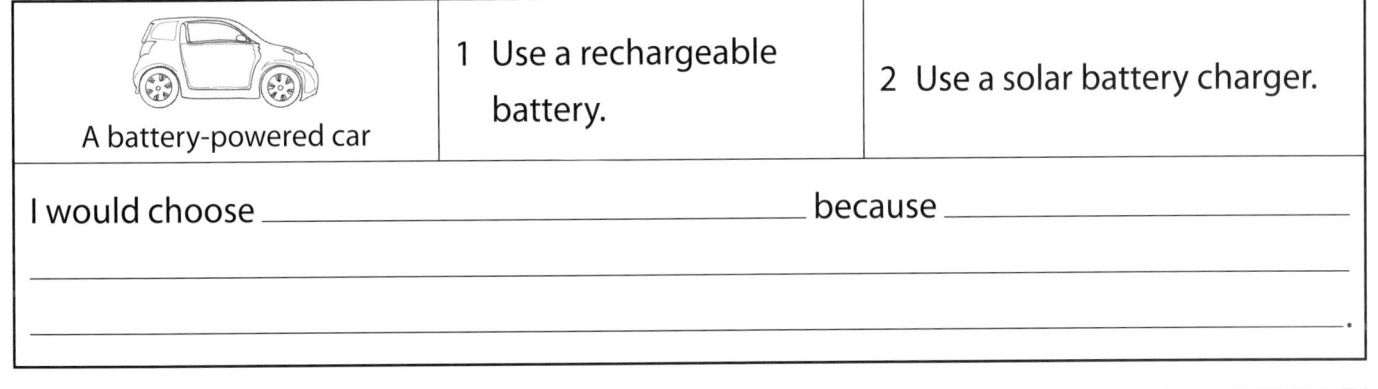

Activity sheet – Alternative choices

Material choices

☞ For each of these projects, choose which material you would use and explain why.

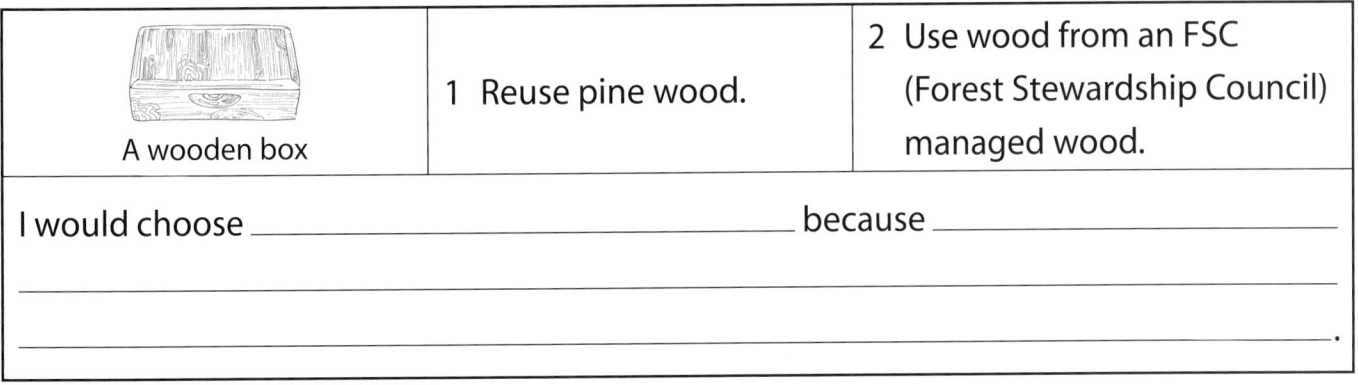

A gift bag	1 Use recycled paper.	2 Create handmade paper.

I would choose _____ because _____

_____

_____ .

Cakes	1 Use a supermarket's own brand of chocolate.	2 Use a brand of chocolate that carries the FAIRTRADE Mark.

I would choose _____ because _____

_____

_____ .

A battery-powered car	1 Use a rechargeable battery.	2 Use a solar battery charger.

I would choose _____ because _____

_____

_____ .

A wooden box	1 Reuse pine wood.	2 Use wood from an FSC (Forest Stewardship Council) managed wood.

I would choose _____ because _____

_____

_____ .

Activity sheet – Alternative choices

Transport choices

When you travel to the local shops, how do you usually get there?

☞ 1 Rank these transport methods from 1 to 6. 1 is the most environmentally friendly way to get to the shops and 6 is the least environmentally friendly way. Explain your answers.

 Scooter	 Car	 Bus
Ranked: _____	Ranked: _____	Ranked: _____
Because: _____	Because: _____	Because: _____
 Walk	 Train	 Taxi
Ranked: _____	Ranked: _____	Ranked: _____
Because: _____	Because: _____	Because: _____

☞ 2 With a partner, discuss the best method of transport to get to Paris.

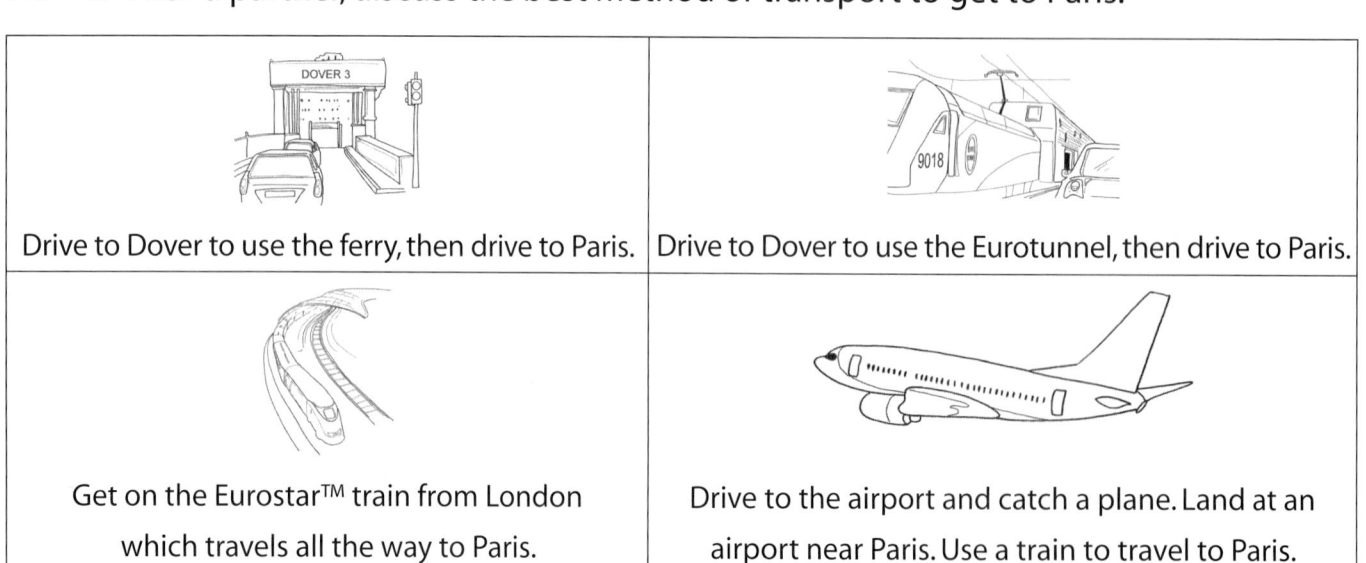

Drive to Dover to use the ferry, then drive to Paris.	Drive to Dover to use the Eurotunnel, then drive to Paris.
Get on the Eurostar™ train from London which travels all the way to Paris.	Drive to the airport and catch a plane. Land at an airport near Paris. Use a train to travel to Paris.

56   Sustainable design   © Folens (copiable page)

Activity sheet – Alternative choices

Build a land yacht

☞ Build a land yacht that uses wind to move it.
You will need:

- Four wheels made from MDF or thick card
- 15cm long axle rods and axle rod holders
- A rectangular piece of corriflute 22cms by 11cms
- Masking tape
- A pencil
- Scissors
- A mast
- A junior hacksaw
- A bench hook
- A plastic carrier bag
- Jumbo art straws

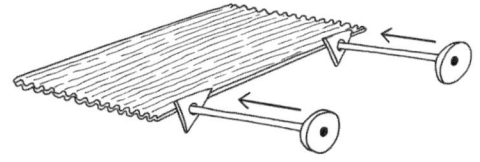

Step 1

Fix the axle rods, wheels and axle rod holders to the corriflute base.

Step 2

Test the wheeled base and make sure it rolls smoothly.

Step 3

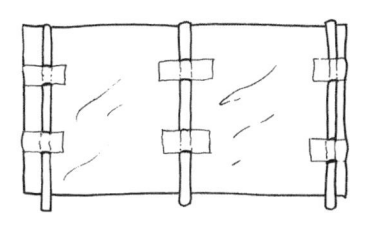

Decide on how big your sail will be. You could use a single mast or up to three masts. Cut the plastic carrier bag into a large rectangle and stick the jumbo art straws into position with masking tape.

Step 4

Use a pencil to make small holes in the base for the mast, or masts, to fit in.

Step 5

Now your land yacht is ready, race it against your classmates or see whose yacht travels furthest with one gust of wind! You could try them out outside or use a fan.

© Folens (copiable page)　　　　Sustainable design　　　　57

Teacher's notes

Product life cycles

Objectives
- To consider what happens to a range of products once they have finished being used
- To understand that some products can have a new life as something else, either by harvesting its materials or by adapting it

Prior knowledge
Students should understand that products break, or that we finish using them. They should have experience of disposing of products in the past.

NC links
Key concepts: 1.1a, 1.1c, 1.1d Designing and making; 1.2 Cultural understanding; 1.3 Creativity
Range and content: b, c, d

Northern Ireland PoS
Designing: b, e, h
Communicating: a

Scottish attainment targets
Technology: Developing informed attitudes – social and environmental responsibility

Welsh PoS
Skills: Designing: 3, 4, 8
Skills: Making: 15

Background
This unit brings together all of the elements from the previous units and looks at what happens to products at the end of their life cycle.

Starter activity
It would be useful to have a class discussion on what students understand by the terms carbon footprint and product life cycle.

Resource sheets and Activity sheets
The Resource sheet, 'Product life cycles', looks at the stages a product goes through from when it is first designed to when it has reached the end of its life. Students can refer to this sheet through the unit to keep the product life cycle stages in mind.

The Activity sheet, 'Carbon footprint', asks students to consider the impact of a carbon footprint and to think about ways in which their own footprint could be reduced. Students could use one of the following carbon footprint calculators: www.carboncontrol.org.uk/carbonator/default.aspa or www.zerofootprintkids.com/kids_home.aspx.

The Activity sheet, 'Lose your bottle', requires students to think about bad habits people have and how they can effect the environment. Students are then asked to design a more environmentally friendly product to help combat a particular wasteful habit. Students will need to have access to empty plastic water bottles and weighing scales.

The Activity sheet, 'The eco-web', asks students to complete an eco-web to determine which areas of a product are not environmentally friendly and could be improved. A completely environmentally friendly product is one that occupies the outside of the web. A product that occupies the inside of the web is thought to be very harmful to the environment. This web is based on the ecodesign web developed by Loughborough University to help students consider sustainability issues when designing and evaluating products. A printable version of the original ecodesign web is available from www.informationinspiration.org.uk/.

The Activity sheet, 'The end?', requires students to consider ways in which products could be used beyond what they were originally designed for. This task draws together the 6Rs to incorporate everything that students have learnt over the last ten units.

Plenary
Ask students to cut a piece of green paper into a leaf shape. On the leaf they should write down three 'green' promises that they will keep over the coming year to reduce their carbon footprint. Use the leaves to create a whole class display on a card tree. Make sure all of the paper used is either recycled or handmade by students!

Resource sheet – Product life cycles

Product life cycles

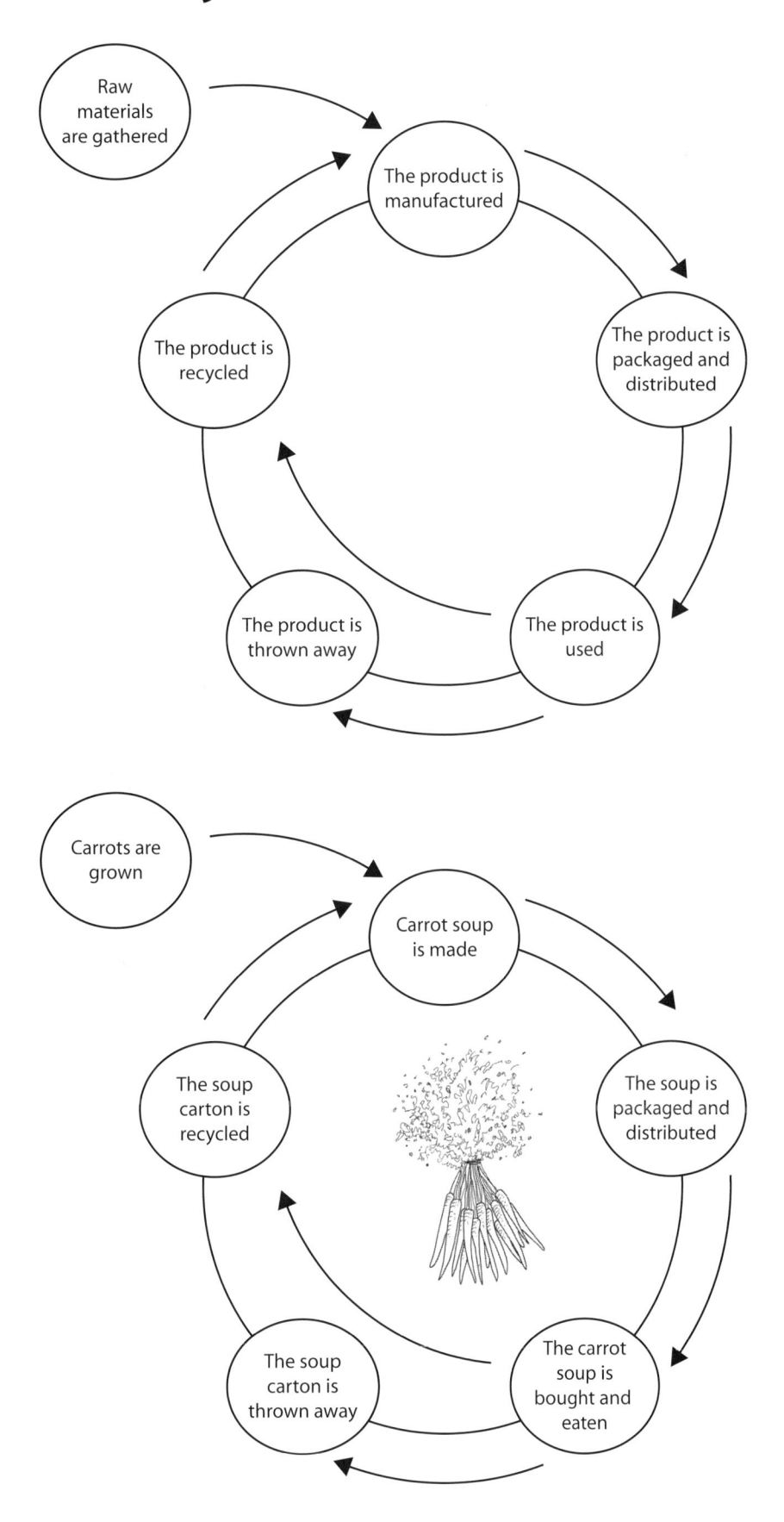

- Raw materials are gathered
- The product is manufactured
- The product is packaged and distributed
- The product is used
- The product is thrown away
- The product is recycled

- Carrots are grown
- Carrot soup is made
- The soup is packaged and distributed
- The carrot soup is bought and eaten
- The soup carton is thrown away
- The soup carton is recycled

© Folens (copiable page)   Sustainable design   59

Activity sheet – Product life cycles

Carbon footprint

A carbon footprint is a way of measuring the impact you have on the environment. The more energy and resources you use, the bigger your carbon footprint is.

☞ 1 Work out your carbon footprint (your teacher will recommend a website).

☞ 2 Design a board game called 'Tread lightly'. Create a grid square. The squares should include a range of 'good green changes', explaining how a person can reduce their carbon footprint. Other squares should explain 'bad wasteful stuff', activities that increase a person's carbon footprint.

☞ 3 Complete the table below with ideas for your board game squares. How many spaces forward or backwards is the item worth to a player? Two examples have been given to help you.

	Good green changes	Number of spaces forward
1	You use energy-saving light bulbs.	1
2		
3		
4		
5		

	Bad wasteful stuff	Number of spaces backwards
1	You leave the tap on when brushing your teeth.	2
2		
3		
4		
5		

Activity sheet – Product life cycles

Lose your bottle

Simon goes to the gym three times a week. Every time he goes he buys a 1 litre bottle of water from the vending machine.

☞ 1 Work out how much plastic Simon is using in a year by completing the table below. You will need to weigh an empty 1 litre water bottle.

Weight of bottle	Number of bottles used per week	Number of bottles used per year	Weight of all the bottles used in a year

☞ 2 Design a reusable bottle that the gym could give away to customers when they join. The gym is called Maximum Health. The water bottle should be comfortable to hold, easy to refill and tell people how much plastic they are saving by not buying bottles.

© Folens (copiable page) — Sustainable design

Activity sheet – Product life cycles

The eco-web

The eco-web helps to compare two similar products to see which is the greenest option. For example, is downloading music 'greener' than buying a CD?

☞ Choose two similar products. For each of the questions around the eco-web, decide how green the product is on a scale of 1 to 5 (1 being very harmful to the environment and 5 being very environmentally friendly.)

If the product is very environmentally friendly, draw a line from that question to the next question in the lightest shaded area (meaning it is 'Very good'). If the product is very harmful to the environment, draw a line from that question to the next question in the darkest shaded area (meaning it is 'Very bad').

Use a different coloured pen for each product.

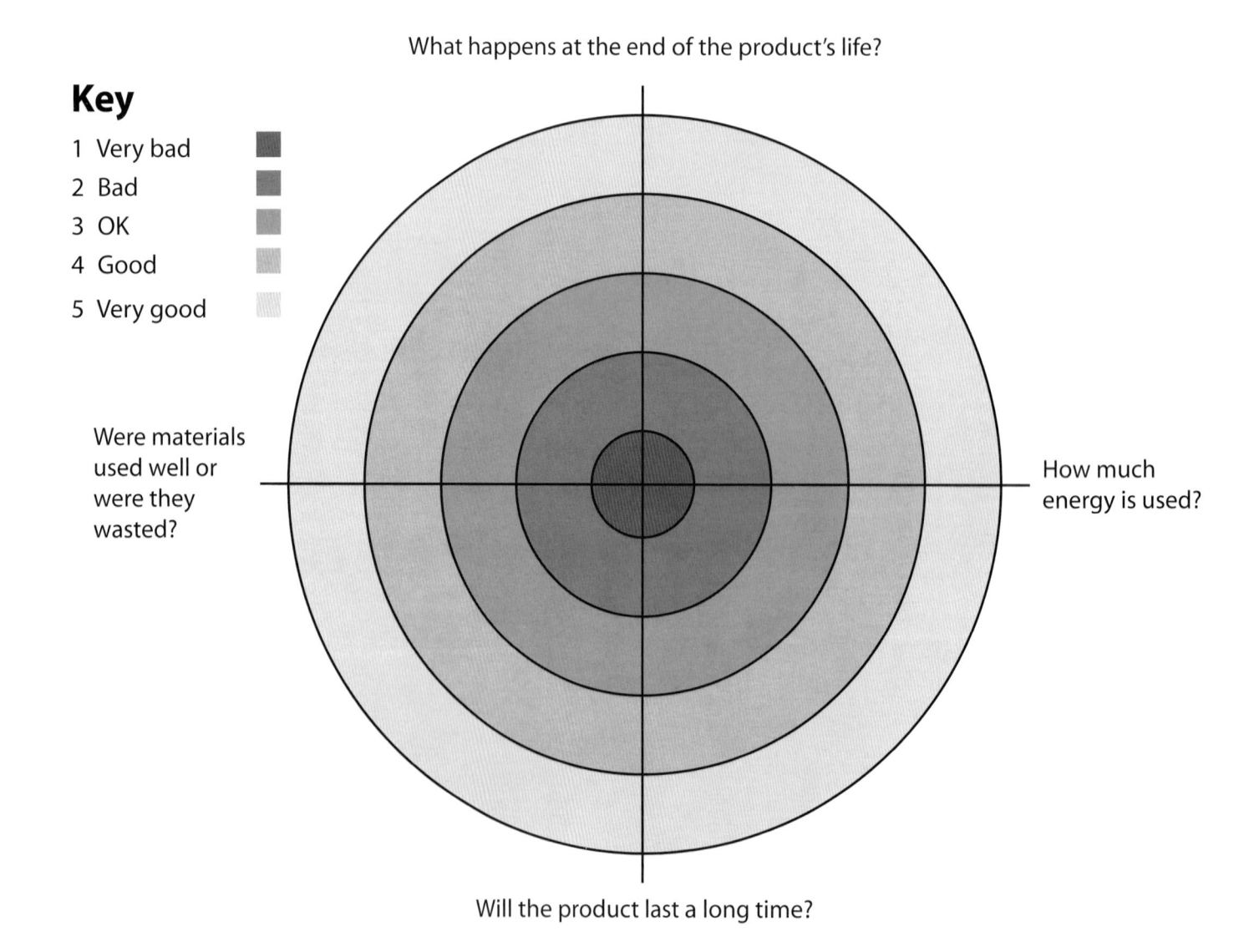

What happens at the end of the product's life?

Key
1 Very bad
2 Bad
3 OK
4 Good
5 Very good

Were materials used well or were they wasted?

How much energy is used?

Will the product last a long time?

Activity sheet – Product life cycles

The end?

When you have finished using a product you should consider the best way to dispose of it.

☞ 1 In pairs, discuss what could happen to each of the following products once they have been finished with, so they continue to be useful. Fill in as many boxes as possible for each item.

Item	Materials it is made from	Reuse it?	Repair it?	Compost it?	Recycle it?	Change it?
A pair of jeans						
A newspaper						
A soft drinks bottle						
A broken CD player						
Vegetable peelings						
A toy a child has grown out of						

☞ 2 Keep a diary of everything you throw away in a week, from Monday to Sunday.

© Folens (copiable page) Sustainable design 63

Assessment sheet – Sustainable design

☞ Fill in the table below to show what you know about the 6Rs.

The 6Rs	This means…	An example of this is…	I have demonstrated this in class (tick)
1 Rethink			
2 Reuse			
3 Recycle			
4 Repair			
5 Reduce			
6 Refuse			

My design meets the 6Rs because: _____

_____

_____

I could improve my design by: _____

_____

_____

One thing I could do to help improve the environment is: _____

_____